A LEARNING
EXPERIENCE

A
LEARNING
EXPERIENCE

by
Mary Bailey

LUCIS PUBLISHING COMPANY
New York

LUCIS PRESS, LTD.
London

First Printing, 1990

ISBN No. 0-85330-139-5

Library of Congress Catalog Card Number: 89-63521

$10/93$

The Lucis Publishing Company is a non-profit orga-
nization owned by the Lucis Trust. No royalties are
paid on this book.

Translation of this title
into Danish, French and German
is proceeding.

MANUFACTURED IN THE UNITED STATES OF AMERICA
BY FORT ORANGE PRESS, INC., ALBANY, N.Y.

TABLE OF CONTENTS

FOREWORD by Mary Bailey

PART I — ALICE AND FOSTER BAILEY

PART II — MY STORY

PART III—A SAMPLING FROM THE PAST

THE GREAT INVOCATION

From the point of Light within the Mind of God
Let light stream forth into the minds of men.
Let Light descend on Earth.

From the point of Love within the Heart of God
Let love stream forth into the hearts of men.
May Christ return to Earth.

From the centre where the Will of God is known
Let purpose guide the little wills of men —
The purpose which the Masters know and serve.

From the centre which we call the race of men
Let the Plan of Love and Light work out
And may it seal the door where evil dwells.

Let Light and Love and Power restore the Plan on Earth.

"The above Invocation or Prayer does not belong to any person or group but to all Humanity. The beauty and the strength of this Invocation lies in its simplicity, and in its expression of certain central truths which all men, innately and normally, accept — the truth of the existence of a basic Intelligence to Whom we vaguely give the name of God; the truth that behind all outer seeming, the motivating power of the universe is Love; the truth that a great Individuality came to earth, called by Christians, the Christ, and embodied that love so that we could understand; the truth that both love and intelligence are effects of what is called the Will of God; and finally the self-evident truth that only through *humanity* itself can the Divine Plan work out."

ALICE A. BAILEY

A LEARNING EXPERIENCE

by Mary Bailey

FOREWORD

It is customary for many people to look back at the end of each year with a critical and evaluating mind, to clear out the rubble and brush away the cobwebs and move into the new year with a clean space ready to receive whatever the future may bring.

Looking back over the events of a lifetime can serve a similar purpose but with a larger horizon and a broader perspective. After more than thirty-three years of service with the group work of the Arcane School and the Lucis Trust, I have found myself looking back, with some nostalgia, and also with the hope that recording some of my group experiences and what was, in fact, a constant learning experience, may have value for others.

There are few left today with any direct personal experience of Alice or Foster Bailey. While she was persuaded to write up part of the events of her own life and work (*The Unfinished Autobiography*), the work, of course, went on after her death in December 1949 with Foster and with others, including myself after about 1950.

This work of Alice's, which was first of all significant because it was hers and depended on her discipleship link with Hierarchy, has acquired a life, a livingness and a significance of its own. It has demonstrated its value to the spiritual Hierarchy in their efforts to stimulate and expand human consciousness,

1

and to the Christ in preparation for his reappearance. As a consequence of this service demonstration, the Arcane School has evolved its group life-line with the great ashram of Sanat Kumara and become a living organism in right relationship with all other organisms within the "great chain of Hierarchy."

This twentieth century marks a decisive and historical turning point in the evolution of human consciousness, a turning point resulting directly from the increased stimulation emanating from the Hierarchy within the directive power of planetary approach to initiation. The work started by Alice and Foster Bailey in 1920 under direct hierarchical impression has always been intended for the stimulation of those changed and changing conditions in consciousness which must be established by the end of this century "to precede and condition the new age."

The teaching given by the Master Djwhal Khul, with Alice's cooperation, is due to achieve its maximum usefulness to disciples and to all seriously motivated men and women of goodwill, during these final years of the century and on into the next. Early in the twenty-first century, the Tibetan expects to conclude the threefold interpretation of the Ageless Wisdom which he had undertaken to present to humanity on behalf of the Hierarchy. The changing and more consistently spiritual attitudes of mind and heart resulting from esoteric teachings thoroughly absorbed, and *lived out in daily life*, should fulfill the purposes of the teachings as expressed in these words from A *Treatise on the Seven Rays, Vol. V* (p. 255): "The remainder of this century . . . must be dedicated to rebuilding the shrine of man's living, to reconstructing the form of humanity's life, to reconstituting the new civilisation upon the foundations of the old, and to the reorganising of the structures of world thought, world politics, plus the redistribution of the world's resources in conformity to divine purpose. Then and only then will it be possible to carry the revelation further."

From these words it is abundantly clear that esoteric teachings, with their subsequent "revelation" in
consciousness, are intended always for factual interpretation and practical use in the everyday world. And
this is made even more evident throughout the books
as one pursues a system of study and meditation. In
fact, esoteric teaching would not have held my own
interest and dedication if it were not so. What a waste
of time and energy to increase and expand one's own
understanding and one's own consciousness if usefulness and service to the evolutionary process is not
the ultimate goal! But for the first time in history
significant numbers of human beings are capable of
self-training for planetary service, of the selfless and
cooperative action discipleship imposes, hence the
availability of these teachings during this twentieth
century—the "hinge" between the old age and the
new. Love of humanity is the keynote; planetary service is the goal.

In the same passage already quoted from *Rays V*,
D. K. states: "In the next century and early in the
century an initiate will appear and will carry on this
teaching. It will be under the same 'impression' for
my task is not yet completed and this series of bridging treatises between the material knowledge of man
and the science of the initiates has still another phase
to run." These words must be coupled with the previous statement, showing clearly that only when we
can use what knowledge and wisdom we have acquired
in creating the new world order of the Aquarian age,
will it *be possible* to carry the teaching further. Evi-
dently the Tibetan *cannot*—and will not—give further teaching and training of such a profound quality
until early next century when the necessary conditions should have been created.

Yet my thirty-three years of experience with this
work emanating from the Tibetan are threaded through
from start to finish with constant claims from a diver-

sity of individuals in different parts. of the world for recognition and acceptance as "channels" or "transmitters" of the Tibetan's new teaching. It had even started while A.A.B. was still alive, but has increased in quantity and in arrogance throughout the years. This is a point I may touch upon, or develop a little, in the course of "looking back", because it is such an ever present reminder of the need for clear thinking and sound discrimination.

Another aspect of the work I hope to develop is the whole matter of present day discipleship. Even with all the teaching we have, this is a little understood and somewhat glamourous concept which we all have to clarify for ourselves.

To open up the central theme of this group work, and to give it the coherence of Foster's unique perspective and inimitable style, a paper of his forms a perfect introduction. I found this paper seven years after his death (in 1977) tucked away in an envelope marked "To be opened only by M.B." Why I had not found this before among the papers I had already sorted out, I simply do not know. But here it is now according to his suggestion that after his death I may wish to publish it. I do so now recognising the reality, the scope and the responsibility of the discipleship Alice and he both manifested in their lives, setting an example few can equal but from which all can benefit.

I am also including at the opening part of these pages some instructions given by the Tibetan to Alice as a means of preparing her for the work he wanted her to do with the books. These papers, too, are among others I was sorting through prior to leaving my desk in the New York headquarters. I am using only part of a large packet of almost daily instructions.

The members of the spiritual Hierarchy give us so much inspiration and help for which we can only be profoundly grateful; but they expect much from us in return and that demands vigilant self-discipline, self-training and, paradoxically, self-forgetfulness, for which comparatively few are ready. Discipleship is no bed of roses for a self-centred personality, but a perfectly natural way of life for a liberated soul.

Mary Bailey

A LEARNING EXPERIENCE

by Mary Bailey

PART I—
Alice and Foster Bailey

CHAPTER 1 — Introduction

The Discipleship of Alice A. Bailey

by Foster Bailey

Alice Bailey is today an active world disciple and a senior member of the ashram of her Master, K.H. She passed on twenty-two years ago this coming December (written in January 1971) and stands free of her etheric and astral vehicles. She now functions on the mental plane in the mental body she had when she died, but that body has been growing ever since. A.A.B. sometimes acts as a personal secretary to K.H. That statement gives us all too inadequate an idea of her relationship to him. She is actively preparing for her next incarnation, which will be soon and which is carefully planned.

Alice's years before her life work emerged are adequately pictured in her autobiography. Many significant and helpful aspects of her discipleship training and work have never been told. I was up close in most all of it, but can say only a little about it.

The present statement is made only as an aid to understanding some aspects of discipleship work at a certain stage. The known personality of A.A.B., as we contacted it, is little involved now. She always detested any spiritual claim-making, and still does, but the record of her discipleship life is available for the aiding of other disciples everywhere. In another month I shall be 83 years of age and I devoutly hope will soon be on my way to subtler realms. (Foster died on June 3, 1977, at 89 years of age. M.B.)

9

What I write now can be published then if Mary thinks it wise. No disciple should take unilateral action on his own affecting the work of another disciple.

For long centuries the occult Hierarchy has been withdrawn from physical plane living as a group, but certain individual Masters have always been in physical bodies working unknown among the sons of men. During this period of withdrawal, soon to end, the Masters worked largely through the disciples they had trained and who, in many cases, were initiates. A.A.B. is such a one.

A.A.B.'s last incarnation was dominated by two objectives, one of which was specifically hers and the other a collaboration with D.K. in his heavy task of providing the bridging teaching needed between the old Piscean age and the new Aquarian era.

She came into incarnation with a fixed purpose of creating a new age esoteric school for discipleship. There was a growing number of aspirants to discipleship with some esoteric knowledge, and this had been greatly augmented by the disciple, H. P. Blavatsky, but there were all too few trained, effective, accepted disciples. If there had been more, the crisis of the world war might have been handled on the mental plane and not precipitated through into physical warfare. The Arcane School was her chosen contribution to hierarchical work and was approved by her Master. Neither K.H. nor D.K. ever controlled her or the creation of the Arcane School. That was her privilege, win or lose.

Her cooperation with D.K. in producing his teaching was quite a different matter. In this she was not free. She wrote what he chose to teach, not what she decided was useful. In the Arcane School she wrote and taught according to her own wisdom. In the later years, as she became saturated with D.K.'s teaching, her mental content enlarged and inevitably what she taught in her School was profoundly affected. There was a most extraordinary and unique blending of A.A.B.'s mental body and the mental body now used by D.K. As she stated, the two pillars supporting all her work were the books and the School.

In all this, my function was, as best I could, to help make all her work successful. I was loaned by M. to D.K. for thirty years. This was a tremendous balancing process for me, neutralising excessive first ray characteristics and opening my heart centre by being in a second ray ashram. I have learned more in this life than in any previous incarnation. Most of all this came to me through A.A.B. Just living so many hours with her was a mental stimulant of great value. She had a second ray soul and a first ray personality. I have a first ray soul and second ray personality. This made a basis for balanced work.

In retrospect, it is clear that A.A.B.'s greatest service was subjective. Those who knew her best and those closer to her personal evolutionary status, knew this full well. Others, perforce, recognised her in terms of physical comings and goings, as a lecturer and by the evidence of physical effects. This subjective potency is naturally true of senior disciples, but we all could increase our constructive effect in the world if we used our auras more consciously and our wills more definitely to meet the subjective needs of those who touch our lives. I have watched Alice time and time again take in inimical forces threatening the Arcane School, sometimes quietly and serenely letting them exhaust themselves against her poise and integrity, and at other times consciously transmuting them. However, she was at times willing to let the group suffer, up to a limited point, for the sake of a brother disciple or because of potential discipleship quality. It takes much wise discrimination to build an esoteric group and a type of impersonality often misunderstood.

One of Alice's outstanding characteristics was the complete absence in her of any desire to control anyone's thinking. She persistently voiced the truth as she understood it, but always opposed the creation of a "Tibetan cult." She practiced repetition, not to convince, but because repetition is necessary to stir sluggish brain cells. This freedom from desire to control left her undisturbed when students left her School.

I have always had periods of discouragement, which I doggedly fought. To help me, D.K. long ago promised that my last days here would be my best, and so it has proved to be. At another time, during World War II, I was discouraged about the future of all the work. D.K. then assured me that the foundations already established would be strong enough for postwar progress. And so also that has proved true. I am indeed a most fortunate man.

The subjective integration of the students in the Arcane School has been rapidly increasing during the last ten years. Our usefulness as a group has become much more real an aid to the Hierarchy. Recognition of spiritual values has deepened and is much more widespread in the group than ever before. The conscious acceptance of a degree of personal responsibility for human welfare has emerged beautifully. The light in the group body has greatly increased. More students in the School know more about world events than was the case only a few short years ago. Our usefulness to the new group of world servers is now emerging. More individual students are making more rapid progress in discipleship consciousness than was the case when Alice passed on. This is because more of us are losing our separateness in service. Our meditation work is steady and strong. Our spiritual studies are enriching our minds. Of the thousands of old souls now incarnated in the youth of the world, a goodly number are joining the School. A.A.B.'s heroic efforts are paying off.

In spite of all the brightness in the above story, the group will not always be sailing calm seas with favourable winds. This is still a tough world to work in, although there is real promise of a better future for all of us.

Workers will become blockage points in the flow of increasing spiritual energies through the group and, in most cases as in the past, will not know it. Personal criticisms are the greatest poisoners of group life. We so often think our critical attitude is justified. Persistent effort to put over one's personal opinions about the group work has spoiled many a young disciple's relations to the group he should work with and blend into. It is hard to be so impersonal as to be able to push on and support what one disagrees with, but group success and greater group usefulness is more important than individual opinions. This I had to learn the hard way this life.

Even when struggling desperately to get bread for her children, Alice spent long hours in the night reading widely and pondering what she read. She studied the *Puranas* and the *Upanishads* of India and the teachings of the *Bhagavad Gita* and of Patanjali. She had at one time collected twenty-six translations of the *Gita*. D.K. had agreed to produce a book with her on the *Gita*, similar to the one on the Yoga Sutras of Patanjali. (The book is *The Light of the Soul*). More pressing work prevented this.

She made a deep study of the writings of Blavatsky and mastered the essentials of the teaching in the *Secret Doctrine*. Her classes on the *Secret Doctrine* and *Isis Unveiled* were gems and her understanding of these two books phenomenal. She browsed in the current theosophical writings, including not only Annie Besant but also Steiner, Tingly, Heindel, Bhagavan Das, and many others. Thus she built a mental foundation and trained herself in clear thinking and wise judgment which enabled her to bring a mind of exceptional quality to D.K.'s work. Her relations to the esoteric section of the Theosophical Society taught her much about esoteric work, particularly some factors which ought not to be. A.A.B.'s efforts to help bring the worldwide theosophical movement on to more useful ground and to increase the esoteric elements in that organisation were hierarchically inspired and a fine preparation for her later work with D.K. D.K.'s work with Alice was much easier for him than his work with H. P. Blavatsky.

With it all she insisted on being a real mother to her three girls, and showed extraordinary patience with me. I learned constantly and much from her. A.A.B. did not have a fifth ray mind, but she was keenly interested in scientific exploration and in the field of theoretical physics. It was only natural that she should give seven lectures in New York on the subject of the atom. As always, she had built a foundation for what she did. She knew a little about the work of such men as Niels Bohr and Rutherford. The book of these New York lectures, under the title, *The Consciousness of the Atom*, has been one of our best sellers for many years.

The actual practical work of building and organising her Arcane School did not really get under way until we had moved to New York in 1920. She had already begun her work with D.K. whom she first contacted in November 1919.

In those days, A.A.B. had achieved the relationship to K.H. known as "Chela on the Thread." That is, she had the privilege of asking for an interview with him. To get through and get an interview which her physical brain could remember, generally took several days. She had such an interview with K.H. who asked her specifically to work with D.K. This overcame all her misgivings and fears. Later, these interviews were superseded by a much closer relationship.

Alice has written of fear as her chief personality failing. She says she feared failure, of having faults, of what people would think of her, of being looked up to, even of the dark. This was a real handicap, which she completely overcame. Her entire astral body was broken down and rebuilt this life, and all of the centres up the spine were opened and functioning. The activity of her heart centre was greatly expanded. But she literally wore out her physical vehicle, and at the last was only kept alive to finish her thirty-year cycle of work with D.K. by monthly blood transfusions. Of these, I took charge under the doctor, of course. It was a great relief when she had worked it all out and could go in December 1949.

Alice made two abortive attempts to find and train her successor to head the Arcane School. The burden therefore fell on me, although it had never been in my schedule. I just had to do the best I could, and we did finally pull through. One headquarters worker was bitterly disappointed. She thought she was entitled to the job, but Alice would not risk it. I had to struggle, but am glad she made that decision. There is a great difference between a glorified probationary path School with old age overtones, and an esoteric discipleship School with new age overtones.

Mary Bailey stands now, and has done so for many years, at the head of the Arcane School and of all our worldwide group work. Her vision is of a new age esoteric discipleship School of increasing usefulness to the Hierarchy and to the Christ. Mary was in preparation for her present job before she contacted esoteric teaching this life, and she joined the Arcane School during the war and before she had met A.A.B. The rays of all of Mary's vehicles are identical with my own. D.K. once said that it is impossible to keep two such people apart in their discipleship work. I have often said, "This is my beloved wife in whom I am well pleased."

Foster Bailey
New York
February 1971

CHAPTER 2—Extracts from D.K.'s Instructions to A.A.B. during 1919

Although the following instructions from D.K. to A.A.B. are not among the earliest ones, I am putting them first here because they explain the methods used by members of the Hierarchy in contacting disciples for service and working with them. They also define the various grades of both hierarchical teachers and receptive disciples, from various perspectives, including the ray influences.

M.B.

I. How the Hierarchy Works in its Relationship with Disciples

Purity of motive and utter fearlessness, with the addition of a profound love of the Master, a longing to serve humanity, are essentials for those who would, as pioneers, break the way for those who follow after.

See to it, therefore, that you cultivate this attitude, for we have no teaching along occult lines for those who strive not this way.

Look not for Masters and angel Devas to write with you, why should they? Only a man with passions such as yours, but a little longer on the Path, seeks thus to help you, not because he cares for you as a person, but because the need is great and you can, and do, teach. We seek to make you more effective and prepare you for other grades of teachers. Be teachable, keep the record and question not until you know more, then question all, discarding that which seems contrary to reason, keeping the residue you can use for the good of the little ones.

Your sentence today is but a brief one; rest mentally upon it, seek out its significance. In years to come you will apprehend what is now withheld.

"The Seven Lights bring each their Light-bearers. They come seven times on each ray, and take their Buddha initiation on their own Light. He Who is coming on the Seventh now takes initiation on the Second."

You ask, brother of mine, as to the method of approach by those of us who teach you on the inner planes, how we come and how we attract and contact your minds. The methods differ according to the status of the teacher. . . . On the inner planes are teachers of all descriptions, some of profound knowledge, others not so much more advanced than those of you who are taught.

I could give you somewhat of this matter and we might divide the information under two headings: 1. Who are thus taught. 2. The methods of communication.

1. *Teaching disciples.*

These methods are the most advanced reached as yet and differ from those employed for the rest of humanity, owing to the fact that a disciple is in the consciousness of his Master and has reached a certain grade or a point of development where his responsiveness is very largely to be depended upon. Certain things must be realised as regards the teaching of a disciple:

(a) The permission of his Master has to be acquired, although the teaching is usually carried out at the request of the Master.

(b) The grade of teachers permitted to contact a disciple is usually of a very high order and, at this particular time in the world's history, a number of very advanced teachers, initiates and high disciples are making a pronounced effort to increase the numbers of those who at this time will take initiation. Their obvious and most fruitful field of endeavour is necessarily among those closely associated with a Master. They can be contacted so easily, and the teaching is more easily apprehended owing to stimulation from being in the Master's consciousness. Full advantage is being taken of this fact therefore.

(c) Disciples can be called most easily by the name of the ego. It is only after the third initiation that a man consciously knows his egoic appellation, but all disciples when freed from the physical body and the physical brain consciousness, respond when called upon.

(d) Disciples who are necessarily engaged upon the work of making the astral body colourless and limpid, like a reflecting mirror, are therefore responsive to colour, and when the teacher seeks to impart information, the basic colour of the ego being known to him, he sounds the note that vibrates to the same measure as that colour, and the sudden flooding of the astral body with the colour sounded (I put it accurately thus) is a sign that the disciple responds.

(e) Disciples who can function on causal levels, who have the causal body consciousness (even though the physical brain registers it not) can be aroused via the ego, again by colour and sound; the ego, with rapidity, calls the attention of the personality.

So, brother, you see how it acts. Disciples can be called:

(a) Via the Master by one close enough to the Master to have that privilege. This is possible only to an initiate.

(b) Via the ego, who transmits the call to the brain of the personality via the atomic subplane.

As you know, to be a disciple at all necessitates a due proportion in the bodies of the atomic subplane matter. It requires causal body consciousness on the part of the disciple.

(c) Directly to the astral body when sufficiently pure. This deals with the transmission of teaching from the buddhic level to the astral and then to the physical brain. It is the highest form of astral psychism and is confined to the atomic subplane. It affects directly the causal body, but is hindered not by the lower mind.

In all this I am dealing with direct conscious communication. I touch not on the teaching given at night or with any of the lower forms of astral psychism. The first kind I will at some later date elucidate. With astral psychism, unless atomic, I never deal.

2. *Advanced egos.*

These are taught somewhat differently. I refer to those nearing the Path, the spiritually inclined, the man of advanced idealism, of altruistic intent, who senses the vision but as yet sees it not. They, too, are watched and known, but the methods of instruction differ.

(a) Telepathically they are called and taught on the plane of the ego. Great teachers and advanced egos, specialists in some particular line, communicate on causal levels and instill the teaching into the ego. This later finds its way into the consciousness of the personality, sometimes at the time of communication, sometimes during the course of the day, often simply as life proceeds, occasionally only in succeeding lives. They are called again by their colour.

(b) Telepathic communication to the physical brain. This method is employed with disciples, too. Only by the grade of teaching can the status of the teacher be apprehended, but the hallmark is sure.

Always by the spoken word and imparted instruction is the point of attainment ever to be known. It is so with you, it is so on higher levels. In speech, the occult creative source, is to be seen the level of achievement. An index sure is it of the age of the soul.

(c) Intuitional suggestion, unknown and unrealised by the man, that leads him to books that teach, that shows him passages of elucidation, that guides him unexpectedly to someone in his environment who can assist him towards fuller knowledge, and that in ways seemingly unimportant increases as the years slip by the aggregate of his mental equipment. Forget not, brother of old, the unremitting care, the zealous watchfulness of all the helpers of the race. The moment a man has equipped his vehicles with matter of the higher subplanes, he becomes a subject of unremitting care to some ego more advanced than himself, later, as progress is made, to some lesser chela, then to some advanced disciple, next to an initiate, until he reaches his Master.

3. *The average man.*

For the average man life teaches, the general atmosphere of endeavour, the driving force of evolution, pushes him on to his goal. Today I deal not with the man of mediocre attainment. Our efforts, in order to more effectively reach him, are being concentrated on the advanced man, on the disciple, and on the earnest striver. They eventually, if we more fully equip them, can reach and permeate the mass.

Disciples and advanced egos receive instruction at this time for two purposes:

1. To test out their fitness for special work in the future, the type of that work being known only to the guides of the race. They test for aptitude in community living, with a view to drafting the suitable ones into the colony of the sixth sub-race; they test for

special lines of work, many incomprehensible to you now, but which as time progresses will become ordinary methods of development; they test for those in whom the intuition has reached a point of development that indicates the beginning of the coordination of the buddhic vehicle or, to be exact, that has reached a point where the molecules of the seventh subplane can be discerned in the aura of the ego. When this is so, they can go ahead with confidence in the work of instruction knowing that certain imparted facts will be apprehended.

2. The second reason instruction is given is that at this time a special group of people have come in all at the same time all over the world to do a special work required at this time—*the linking up of the two planes, the physical and the astral via the etheric.* This sentence is important for it is a specific definition of the work that you all have come in to do. In this linking up of the two planes, people are required, as aforesaid, who, being polarised in their mental bodies, or being well rounded out and balanced if not polarised there, can work with intelligence under us in the development of this work. It necessitates primarily people in whose vehicles can be found a proportion of matter of the atomic subplane, so that direct communication can be effected via the atomic cross-section of the causal body. I have digressed thus for the purpose of rendering clear in your minds the fact of who is taught and why.

The Teachers. Always remember, brother of mine, that in the Hierarchy naught is lost through failure to recognise the law of economy. Every expenditure of force is subjected to wise foresight and discrimination. You do not put a university professor to teach the first grade in your schools, and in like manner, we do not put our advanced teachers to instruct the beginners. All progresses under law and order and wise judgment.

Know you that each of you is recognised by the brilliance of his light. This is an occult fact. The finer the grade of matter built into the bodies, the more brilliantly shines forth the indwelling light. Light is vibration after all, and in the measurement of vibration comes the grading of the scholars. Hence nothing can retard a pupil but his own negligence, and nothing can prevent his progress forward if he but attend to the purification of the matter of his bodies. The light within shines forth with ever greater clarity as the refinement proceeds; when atomic matter predominates, great is the glory of the inner man.

Remember, therefore, that you are all graded, if I may so express it, according to the magnitude of the light, according to the rate of vibration, according to the purity of the tone of the ego, according to the clarity of the colour. All these terms express a synonymous fact and state in analogous terms the altitude in evolution achieved by the man. According to this grading, so the teacher. Similarity of vibration holds the secret. Groups of egos are formed:

(a) According to their ray.

(b) According to their sub-ray.

(c) According to their rate of vibration.

They are also grouped:

1. As egos according to the egoic ray and age.

2. As personalities according to the monadic sub-ray (which as you have been told governs the personality; every personality is on one sub-ray of the monadic ray) and according again to the measure of vibration of the subtler bodies and the refinement of the physical. All are graded and charted.

These great charts are under the care of the Chohan of a ray, each ray having its own collection of charts, though each being in many sections (dealing with incarnate, discarnate, and perfected egos). Each section is under the care of subordinate guardians. The Masters have their great Halls of Records with a system of tabulation incomprehensible to you owing to its magnitude and necessary intricacies, wherein the charts are kept. The great Lipika Lords with their vast bands of helpers are the most frequent users of the charts, and many of the discarnate egos awaiting incarnation or having just left the earth, sacrifice their time in devachan to assist in this work. These great Halls of Records are mostly on the lowest level of the mental plane, and the highest of the astral, as they can there be most fully utilised and are most easily accessible. To return to those who teach and who they teach:

Initiates receive instructions direct from the Masters, or from some of the great devas. These teachings are usually imparted at night in small classes or individually (if the occasion warrants it) given in the Master's study. This applies to initiates in incarnation or on the astral plane. If on causal levels, they receive instruction at any time deemed advisable direct from the Master to the causal body.

Disciples are taught occasionally in groups in the Master's larger classes held in their ashrams, at night if in incarnation. Apart from these occasional though regular gatherings to receive direct teaching from the Master, on very rare occasions a disciple, for some specific reason, may be called to the Master's study for a private interview. This eventuates when a Master wishes to see a disciple for commendation, warning, or to decide if initiation is desirable. All this with a view to the disciple's helpfulness to the many. The major part of a disciple's tuition is left in the hands of some initiate or more advanced disciple who watches over his younger brother and is responsible to the Master for his progress, having to hand in regular reports. Karma is largely the arbiter of this relationship.

Just at present, owing to the need, a slightly different policy is being pursued and an intensified training is being given to some disciples by some Masters of the Lodge who have not hitherto taken pupils; the press of work on the Masters who do take disciples being so great, they have delegated some of their most promising pupils to some other Masters, drafting them into small groups for a brief period. The experiment is being tried of intensifying the teaching and of subjecting disciples, not initiates, to the strong vibration of the Master. Ponder on this. It involves risk but if successful tends to the greater assisting of the race.

Classes are held by initiates of the first and second degrees for accepted disciples, for those on the probationary path, between the hours of ten and five every night in all parts of the world, so that the continuity of the teaching is complete. They gather in the Hall of Learning, and the method is much the same as in the big universities—classes at certain hours, experimental work, examination work, and a gradual moving up. A number of egos on the Probationary Path are in the department that is analogous to the high school; others have matriculated and are in the university itself; graduation eventuates when initiation can be taken; the initiate passes from the Hall of Learning to the Hall of Wisdom.

Advanced egos, the spiritually inclined men, attend instruction from disciples, and on occasions the large classes conducted for their benefit by initiates. Their work is more rudimentary, though occult from a worldly standpoint, and they learn under supervision to be invisible helpers. The invisible helpers are gathered mostly from amongst the advanced egos. The very advanced, those on the Path, work more frequently in what might be termed departmental work, forming assistants to the Hierarchy, even though not yet belonging to it.

Three great departments of instruction watch over three parts of man's development:

1. Instruction is given tending to the disciplining of the life, the growth of character, the development (if I may put it so) along cosmic lines of the microcosm. The man is taught the meaning of himself, he comes to know himself as a complex, complete unit, a replica in miniature of the outer world. In the learning of the laws of his own being comes comprehension of the one self and a realisation of the basic laws of the system.

2. Instruction is given as to the macrocosm, the simplification of his intellectual apprehension of the working of the cosmos; instruction as to the kingdoms of nature, teaching as to the laws of those kingdoms, information as to the working of those laws in all the kingdoms on all planes, and a general deep fund of knowledge, of facts, of data, is gradually acquired by him. He finds the macrocosm by way of the microcosm, but when he reaches his own periphery he is met by those who lead him on to encyclopedic knowledge. Remember, he knows not everything, but the way to know, the sources of knowledge, the reservoirs of information, are in his hands. A Master can at any time find out anything on any possible subject without the slightest difficulty.

3. Instruction is given in what I might term *synthesis*. This type of information is only possible as the buddhic vehicle corrdinates. It is really the occult apprehension of the Law of Gravitation or Attraction (the basic Law of this, the second, system) with all its corollaries. He learns the meaning of occult cohesion, of that internal unity which holds the system as a separated unit. This instruction is given principally after the third initiation.

Let me see if I can suggest for you the usual procedure, asking you nevertheless to remember that no hard and fast rules can be laid down, for individuals differ so radically.

Before the first initiation, while the man is on the probationary path, he is taught principally to know himself, to ascertain his weaknesses and to correct them; he is taught to work as an invisible helper first, though is later moved on to more selected work; he is taught the rudiments of the Divine Wisdom; he is entered into the great Hall of Learning; he is known to a Master and is in the care (for definite teaching) of a disciple or, if of rare promise, of an initiate.

After the first initiation he is taught principally the facts anent the astral plane; he has to stabilise his astral body and to learn to work on the mental plane with the same facility and ease that he does on the physical; he is brought in contact with the astral devas; he learns to control the astral elementals; he functions with facility on the various subplanes and passes out of the Hall of Learning into the great Hall of Wisdom. At the same time his mental equipment grows, though emphasis is laid on his astral development.

After the second initiation the teaching shifts up a plane. He learns to control his mental vehicle perfectly; he perfects his control of thought matter and learns the laws governing creative thought building; he functions freely on the four lower subplanes of the mental plane, and before the third initiation he must — consciously and unconsciously — be complete master of the four lower subplanes in each of the three worlds. His knowledge of the microcosm advances towards perfection; he has mastered theoretically the laws of his own nature and experimentally has perfected the control of the four lower subplanes on all the three lower planes. I emphasise this matter as it is of interest. The control of the three higher subplanes is not yet complete, and hence you have the explanation of the failures of an initiate. His mastery of matter is yet incomplete in the three higher planes; they remain to be dominated.

At the third initiation the personality has reached a point where its vibration is of a very high order, its matter in all the three bodies relatively pure, and its

apprehension of the work to be done in the microcosm and the share he is to take in the work of the
macrocosm is very advanced.

After the third initiation the work is intensified,
and the mastering and accumulation of knowledge
has to be unbelievably rapid. The initiate has frequent
access to the libraries of occult books, and after this
initiation he can not only contact the Master with
whom he is linked and whom he has known consciously
for some time, but can contact and assist in his measure, the Chohans, the Great Lord, and His Brother.
He has to grasp the laws of the three lower planes
intellectually, and likewise wield them for the aiding
and carrying out of the great evolutionary schemes.
He studies the cosmic planes and has to master the
charts; he becomes versed in occult technicalities,
develops fourth dimensional vision if it has not hitherto been an instrument he can use; he learns to direct
the activities of the building devas and to cooperate
with the greater Devas, and at the same time and
always he develops his spiritual nature. He begins to
coordinate the buddhic vehicle rapidly and in its coordination he develops the power of synthesis, at first
in small measure and gradually in fuller detail. By
the time the fourth initiation is reached, he has mastered perfectly the fifth subplane and is adept—to
use a technical phrase—in the five lower subplanes in
the three worlds and is well on the way to master the
sixth. His buddhic vehicle can function on the two
lower subplanes of the buddhic.

After the fourth initiation not much remains to be
done. The domination of the sixth subplane proceeds
with rapidity, and the matter of the higher subplanes
of the buddhic is coordinated. He is admitted into
closer fellowship in the Lodge and his contact with
the devas is more complete. He is rapidly exhausting
the resources of the Hall of Wisdom, and is mastering
the most intricate plans and charts, is adept in the

significance of colour and sound, can wield the laws
in the three worlds, can contact his monad with more
freedom than the majority of the human race can contact their ego, and is in charge himself of large work,
teaching many pupils, aiding in many schemes, and
correlating and gathering together under him those
who are to assist him in future times.

I deal here with those who stay to help human evolution on this planet. With those who pass on to
other work I deal not today. Later I may enlarge upon
the matter.

After the fifth initiation the man is perfected as far
as this scheme goes, though he may, if he will, take
two further initiations.

To achieve *the sixth initiation*, he has to take a
very intensive course in planetary occultism. A Master wields the Law in the three worlds; a Chohan of
the sixth initiation wields the Law in the Planet, while
a Chohan of *the seventh initiation* wields the Law in
the system. Beyond this I may not take you for it
concerns you not; the paths of service being many,
specialists in their various departments progress
diversely and the complication in your mind would
be too much.

II. Problems and Attitudes of Disciples

This is the point that I seek today to make clear.
*Personalities warring against ego are doomed even-
tually to lose.* The strong vibrations of those acting
under control of the ego will inevitably beat out those
of the personalities. Forget not, brother of mine, that
the patience and staying power of the ego is long tried
and is bound to succeed. What you who strive for the
good of the whole and in line with the force that makes
for evolution need to do is to keep the channel clear
so that the ego can impress the consciousness ade-

quately. Nothing but good can come from the higher Self; it harbours no evil. Therefore, when unscrupulous action takes place, when wrong words are spoken, when evil and false motives are imputed, then sure is the recognition that the personality only is involved.

I have words of serious import. I waste not time in prefaces and in soft covering of my thoughts; I speak to you plainly. I can, for well we know that what we say will be apprehended by you and acted upon.

You are hindering your usefulness and arresting our opportunities to use you as a channel, through the harbouring of *fear*. It causes strong vibrations in the emotional vehicle, and you must remember, in practice and not just in theory, that if the astral body is in a whirl it hinders communication between the ego and the personality. The astral body acts as an intermediary for the transmission of thought. If it, therefore, is fluctuating and vibrating violently to fear (which is your special failing; with others it may be desire, or anger, or jealousy), nothing can pass from higher levels and impinge upon the physical brain, for in its passage down it will contact the strong vibration of the astral body and be thrown violently back.

You are beginning to develop the intuition; remember that the astral body and the intuitional plane are peculiarly allied. Much as we seek to use you as a transmitter of ideas from the Triad, we cannot do so unless you have a calm, quiet, placid astral body. Test after test is being sent you, and will continue to be sent, until you have either learned the lesson necessary or we perceive that we must wait to use you in a future incarnation.

Eliminate fear, doubt, worry, and see if your usefulness and the development of that inner source of inspiration that you are beginning to tap does not increase in a wonderful manner. Do not dry up that source of information through your own uncontrolled emotional nature. You can control the astral body. How?

1. *By direct inhibition.* This method you have used to advantage in the past. You learned to do it when quite young. It was necessary then, but now it is not the best method for you to use. It reacts on the physical body, leading to congestion in the astral vehicle and then to a similar condition in the etheric. Hence, the headaches to which you have been so prone. Discontinue this method.

2. *By direct realisation of the issues at stake* and the consciousness that, for a pupil of the Master, nothing comes but what leads to development and increased usefulness. You have always admitted the development aspect, believe now the other. Fear with you is not based on timidity (a paradoxical statement). It is based on pride. Being polarised in the mental body, your fear is allied to your intellect. It is, therefore, harder to overcome than the fear of the person polarised in the astral body. They can bring the intellect to bear on its elimination; you have directly to call in the ego. Always the higher to crush out the lower. Hence the necessity for always keeping the channel clear. Do not crush out fear; force it out by the dynamic power of.substitution. This leads to my third suggestion that you cure the fear habit by—

3. *A direct method* of relaxation, concentration, stillness, and flushing the entire personality with pure white light. Proceed thus: You are, we will say, in a state of panic, suggestions of great unpleasantness are crowding in, your imagination runs riot and your mind enforces the riot. Forget not that the fears of an emotional person are not so potent as yours, for this reason, that having a strong mental body you clothe your fear thoughts with mental matter, highly vitalised, which causes a powerful thoughtform to be created, which circulates between you and the cause of your fear and brings probably to pass the disaster feared.

You, realising this, deliberately will seek quietness. You will relax your physical vehicle, quiet by the method previously learned — only very temporarily — your astral vehicle, and steady the mind as far as may be. Then, visualising yourself — the personality, the ego and your Master as the highest apex of the triangle — you will call down a stream of pure white light and, pouring it through all your lower vehicles, cleanse away all that hinders. Continue this process until you realise that the needed work is accomplished. At first you may have to do it many times. Later, just once will suffice and, later still, the whole process may be needless for you will conqueror be.

This applies to the fears connected with the personality. You use the love aspect, flooding yourself with love and light.

Legitimate fears arising not from things connected with the personality, but from the circumstances of the work to be done and from the knowledge of materialised obstructions to the work, must be treated somewhat differently. Here again you follow a definite method:

(a) Still the physical body.

(b) Quiet, by temporary inhibition, the astral body.

(c) Link up with the ego and definitely reason out the proper method of procedure in meeting the difficulty. Having exhausted all the higher rational methods, and clearly seen your course of action, you then —

(d) Raise your vibration as high as may be and call down from the intuitional levels added light on the situation. If your intuition and reasoning faculty in meeting produce harmony, then proceed, knowing as an occult fact past your altering — a law immovable — that nothing can happen but what is for the best. You are being guided and he who sees the end from the beginning makes no error.

A third class of fears, which you will contact ever more as the years go by, are based on the realisation of the occult forces at work on the dark side. Occult attacks and occult powers manifesting in unexpected manner will occur and be directed against all the various vehicles of those who work on our side, sometimes one vehicle and sometimes another being the object of attack; sometimes, in rare cases and where the worker is important enough, on all at once. Sometimes attacks will be directed at individuals, sometimes at groups.

To counter them you employ the first method, with these additions and changes. Link yourself up—either as an individual or forming one of a group—with the ego and *with the Lodge*, not simply with your Master but with the Brotherhood for whom you are working. Then, when stillness has been achieved, you visualise those Masters you know of and, raising your vibration higher still, you connect up with the Chohans— the great Lord and the Manu, according to the line, religious or political, along which the attack comes. You then pour through the linking chain, and through all vehicles, the light of violet that comes in with this ray, and nothing can then stand. This method is only for use when dire the need and great the necessity.

The matter is vital. Guard it well for I have not the time to waste in ceaseless repetition.

Always, as one approaches nearer to the Master, it is, as says *Light on the Path*, with "feet bathed in the blood of the heart." Always each step upward is through sacrifice of all that the heart holds dear, and always must it be voluntary. Some ask for the test and go through it with eyes open, souls they are who in former lives have stepped upon the Path. Others, as Job, go forward blindly trusting, accepting the seeming blows of an unreasonable fate as the instrument in the hands of a wise creator. Suffering with sight and comprehension is easier than the blind acquiescence that accepts, and learns, and trusts.

Look you how comes it to pass. Try and hear with exactitude for I seek to enlighten . . .

It is not necessary to produce the synthetic faculties of clairvoyance and clairaudience until after the third initiation, the first at which the Lord and King, the Ruler, contacts the initiate. Three things have to be accomplished, the reason for which will be apparent.

At the first initiation the control of the ego over the physical body must have reached quite a high degree of attainment, The "sins of the flesh," as the Christian phraseology has it, must be dominated; no longer will the physical elemental demand, and find its demand obeyed; the control must be complete and the lure departed. A general attitude of obedience to the ego must be achieved and the willingness to obey must be very strong. At this initiation the control of the ego is increased; the channel of communication expanded, and physical plane obedience becomes practically automatic. I speak of full achievement; there are degrees as egos differ. Sacrifice and the death of the physical is the point aimed at.

At the second initiation a similar process has been attained as regards the astral body. Desire itself is dominated by the ego, and only that longed for which is for the good of the whole and in line with the will of the ego and the Master. The astral elemental is controlled, the astral body has become pure and limpid, and all dies that is of the lower nature. At the second initiation the ego grips afresh the two lower bodies and bends them to his will. The aspiration and the longing to serve and love and progress becomes so strong that achievement becomes more rapid, which accounts for the fact that the second and the third initiations frequently follow each other in one single life. At this period of the world's history such stimulus has been given to evolution that aspiring souls, sensing the great world's dire and crying need, are sacrificing all in order to meet that necessity. The physical body and the desire nature being disciplined and controlled, what is the next step; the bringing of the mental body on the four lower levels into line also.

Make not the mistake, brother of mine, of thinking that all this follows in consecutive steps or stages. Much is done in simultaneous unison, for slow and hard the labour for control; but between the first three initiations some definite point in each body's evolution has to be acquired before the expansion of the channel can safely be permitted. Many of you are working on all three bodies now.

Before the third initiation a large measure of thought control must be attained, the thoughtforms created must be clear and well defined, not coloured by the lower mind and desires, but pulsating with the spirit of service; not given to the non-essentials of life and the frivolities of the lower mind but consecrated to tile principles of altruism and striving after unity; not disjointed and uncorrelated, but attaining a fair measure of synthesis.

Hard and ceaseless must the work be before this can be done, but when the desire nature is controlled first, the control of the mind body comes more easily. The path of the bhakti is easier than that of the intellectual for they have learned a measure of purified desire and progress by the requisite stages.

Then see you now, my brother, the reason why it is only at the third initiation that the great Hierophant Himself officiates? Earlier the initiate could not stand in His Presence; only the fully consecrated physical body can safely bear the vibrations of the two other bodies when they return to its shelter from the Presence of the King. Only the purified astral body and controlled mental body can safely stand before Him. When purified and controlled they STAND, and for the first time consciously vibrate to the ray of the Monad. Then with prepared bodies, consecrated and controlled can the ability to see and hear on all the three planes be granted and achieved; can the faculty of reading and comprehending the records be permitted, for with fuller knowledge comes added power and can full and waking consciousness be allowed for the heart is sufficiently pure and loving, and the intellect sufficiently stable to stand the strain of KNOWING. Ponder and digest.

―――――――――――

Brother of mine, in silence lies security and the wise working out of the Master's plans. ... What those who guide humanity need just now, as always, are silent, strong transmitters, those whose minds can seize upon the thought and wish as expressed by the Brothers, and transmit them in adequate fashion for the good of the little ones. It matters not to your hearers where the knowledge comes from. What their intuition recognises as true they absorb and use, and the betterment of the race to just that amount is effected. Sincerity is what appeals, and the faculty of impressing your hearers with the accuracy of the imparted statements. This can only eventuate from your own strong inner convictions.

Much concern is being felt among many of you as to the guarding of thought and the protection of the formulated idea or suggestion. Let me give some practical help. Some thoughts and ideas clothe in mental matter and keep their habitat on the plane of thought matter. Such are the abstract conceptions and the scarcely sensed facts of the inner, occult or mystic life that pass through the mind of the thinker. Not so difficult to guard are they, for their vibrations are so high and light that few people have the power to clothe them adequately in mental matter, and those few are so very scarce that the risk of such statements being unwisely promulgated is not very great.

Then there are the communications involved in occult teaching. The circle of those who apprehend them is widening somewhat and these thoughtforms frequently take to themselves astral plane matter from the desire in the heart of the student to verify, corroborate and share with the group whose knowledge is as vital as his. Sometimes this may be, and sometimes maybe not. If prohibited, what is the method of protection then? Largely, brother of mine, a refusing to allow the matter of the astral plane to adhere to the mental thoughtform. Fight the matter out on the desire level and inhibit that from formulating. Where the desire to speak exists, and where the striving is to prevent the gathering of the material around nucleus, another thoughtform is built up, one that intervenes and protects.

Still another type of thoughtform comes forth, the most prevalent and the one that causes the most trouble. These are the facts of information, the detailed material, the news (if so you like to call it), the basis of what may degenerate into gossip that concerns either your work, administrative or otherwise, and other people. How shall you prevent your mind from transmitting to another some fact such as I suggest? It is a fact that has its origin in a physical plane occurrence, and therein lies your difficulty. The inner facts of the occult life, and those that originate on the mental plane are not so difficult to hide. They come not your way until your vibrations are keyed high enough for them and, as a rule, when that is so, character of sufficient stability and wisdom goes alongside. But it is not thus with a physical plane fact. What must be done?

The other thoughts from above arise; these latter from the physical plane work upwards and are increased in vitality by the knowledge of the many, often of the many unwise. One kind starts nebulously on the mental plane and only the higher type of mind can formulate it and clothe it with matter in geometrical precision. Such a mind usually has the wisdom that refuses to clothe it in astral plane matter. Not so with the physical plane fact; it is a vital entity, robed in material of the astral plane and the mental plane when first you meet and contact it. Will you vitalise it, or will you arrest it? Arrest it, brother of mine, by a rush and wave of love for the party implicated that envelops the thoughtform and sends it back to the originator, borne on the wings of a rush of astral plane matter strong to sweep through and around, mayhap disintegrating, but most certainly returning it harmlessly to the sender. Mayhap, too, it is an evil piece of information, a lie or lies of gossip. Devitalise it by love, break it in pieces by the power of a counter thoughtform of peace and harmony.

Or again it may be true, some sad or evil occurrence or deed of some mistaken brother. What then is there to do? Truth cannot be devitalised or disintegrated; the Law of Absorption will aid you here. Into your heart you absorb the thoughtform you encounter, and there transmute it by the alchemy of love. Let me be practical and illustrate, for the matter is of importance.

Some brother comes to you and tells you a fact about another brother, a fact involving what the world would call wrongdoing on that brother's part. You who know so much more than the average man of the street will realise that the so-called wrongdoing may be but the working out of karma, or have its basis in a good motive wrongly construed. You add not to the talk, you hand not on the information; where you are concerned the thoughtform built around the fact has wandered into what you call a cul-de-sac.

What do you then? A counter stream of thoughts you build which, on a wave of love, you send your apparently erring brother, thoughts of kindly assistance, of courage and inspiration, and of a wise application of the lessons to be learned from the deed he has accomplished, using not force, for strong thinkers must not unduly influence other minds, but a gentle stream of wise transmuting love. You see three methods I advise, none strictly occult, for these shall be imparted later, but methods available for the many. Teach them.

1. The thoughtform kept to mental levels, *i.e.*, the inhibiting of astral plane matter.

2. The thoughtform broken up, disintegrated by a stream of love force well directed.

3. The absorbing of the thought form, and the formulation of a counter thought of loving wisdom.

Inhibition: Disintegration: Absorption.

Discouragement, brother of mine, is due to three causes. I seek to elucidate. I am endeavouring just now to help you to eliminate certain attributes in your disposition that make your life harder and impair your usefulness. The work these days is heavy; few there be who serve. These few must be disciplined and developed so they may make of themselves the value of two average workers. I seek for a time to help you. Discouragement, therefore, may be traced to three causes:

1. Paramountly to physical fatigue, to the lowering of the vitality of the bodily organism. When such is the case, the astral body makes too strong a demand on the physical and, in the endeavour to respond and the sensed incapacity to adequately do so, lies the cause of the sense of discouragement. This often attacks those of you who are finely organised in the physical vehicle. The cure for this type of discouragement is obvious, is it not? Rest and relaxation builds anew and gives time for nature to adjust the matter of the vehicle. The sun also revitalises with prana and this is to be recommended. Brother of mine, after all, sound common sense is the special requirement,

and a realisation that one's work is but proportionate to one's capacity, and not to the overwhelming need. Meditate on this.

2. Another basis for discouragement is the over-development of the concrete mind which makes too great demands on the desire body, and incidentally thus on the physical vehicle. Too great a capacity to grasp the entirety of a subject, too disproportionate a comprehension of the world's need, too easy an apprehension of the many issues involved in connection with some particular matter, causes a violent vibration in the astral body which leads to a shattering of the physical body, and this is termed by you discouragement. It is here, brother of mine, that a sense of proportion must be cultivated, that the faculty of wise balancing enters, that mental equilibrium must be sought for. The cure here very largely lies in the realisation that time, eternity, evolution (call it what you will) brings all things to pass and that all depends not on individual effort. Possible it is for wise souls to hasten but nevertheless the end is sure; if the wise souls are not forthcoming yet the force in evolution brings all to pass. Forget this not, but when discouragement from mental sources settles down in quietness, adjust yourself, and in contemplation sense the ultimate achievement of that great factor, time.

3. A third cause lies in more occult sources and comes from the pairs of opposites. When swings the pendulum towards that which you call dark, evil, undesirable, it causes those of you who strive towards the light a tension that results in discomfort in all the bodies and is especially sensed as depression or discouragement in the physical body. It is a weapon applied by the dark brothers to cause a letting up of the activities of the worker for the Light. Much they use it, and the more the sensitiveness of your body grows and the greater your responsiveness to the finer forces, will come this form of temptation. It is one of

the things that hinders. It renders you negative and receptive, it slows down your vibration, it prevents your achieving much, and the little ones suffer.

The cure for this discouragement lies not in cultivating a violent counter vibration, it lies not in inhibition or the building of a separating wall. It lies:

(a) In the wise use of the mental body. A capacity to reason logically and to see the cause of conditions in your own personality or in your environment results in the attainment of poise.

(b) As aforesaid, in the appreciation of the faculty of time as a solvent.

(c) In the stilling then of the concrete mind and the subsequent linking up with the ego and, via the egoic channel, with the Master. Forget not that contact with the Master comes that way, and that he who comes more and more under the guidance of the ego is he who more and more enters into the consciousness of his Master.

Then, having with unselfish intent linked up with the Master, with deliberation and concentration, the effort to work with dispassion, and with no desire to see the fruits of action comes next, and this process, long continued, will result eventually in an equilibrium that nothing can disturb.

Ponder on this and seek to follow my suggestion in this matter.

————————

I presume that some day you will all learn wisdom in the management of your lower vehicles. If you wish to continue to work for us, and if you wish to act as intermediaries between us and the world, you must seek to make your lowest vehicle in shape to receive and transmit. This involves steady nerves, a well rested and nourished body, no mental tension, an astral body clear, limpid and still. When the physical is not in good condition, it involves the other two in its downfall; your apprehension of my words is therefore not clear or accurate. I dare not come and dictate to you, and your astral poise is such that one must not approach you for fear of causing an over-vibration that might shatter quite seriously the physical. All the bodies intermingle and interact on each other and, as said the initiate Paul, "If one member suffers, all the other members suffer with it."

Instructions I give you not on this matter of physical health, for the mistakes you make are not those of theory but of practice. What is simply needed is a working out in daily practice of that wise discrimination that should distinguish all who are linked with us. I have no more to say on this subject save to conjure for the sake of a needy world to do only that which you know to be necessary, to refuse work that comes not directly from the Master, to accept nothing in the nature of extra work without twenty-four hours due consideration, and should this not be granted be sure therefore that the Master's wish is not in it. He never rushes his workers into office or into duties without the time to consider and count the cost. Above all, rest, and seek solitude. In solitude the rose of the soul flourishes; in solitude the divine self can speak; in solitude the faculties and graces of the higher self can blossom in the soil of the personality; and in solitude the Master himself can approach and impress upon the quiescent soul the knowledge that he seeks to impart, the lesson that needs to be learned, the wish of his that should be fulfilled, the method and plans for work that he seeks the disciple to grasp, for through human instruments he has to work, and he is much handicapped by failure on their part.

Think, brother of mine, how it must be with them. In conclave wise they make their plans, in judgment proved they apportion the tasks. Then to those set apart for service they seek to transmit as much of the Plan as possible. They go to some man or some woman on the physical plane and impress their wishes on the mind. If that mind is unstable, or over-satisfied, filled with pride, or with despair; if the emotional body violently vibrates to some rhythm set up by the personality, or if the physical vehicle ails and concentrated attention is therefore prevented, what happens? The Master turns sadly away, distressed to think of the opportunity for service the worker has lost through his own fault, and he seeks someone else to fill the gap, someone perhaps not so fundamentally suited, yet the only one available on account of the first one's failure.

Another thing, brother of mine, remember this— much of the work done by many of you is the result of over-zealousness, not the carrying out of the Master's work. He with wise discrimination apportions the work and never on any one person lays more than he can accomplish. He can and does train so that it seems as if one man accomplishes miracles but, forget not, the vast amount of work accomplished by one useful disciple is only possible when the control of all three bodies is very largely accomplished.

He who has a mental body stable and strong, positive to receive from above, negative to all lower vibration, he who has an astral body clear, uncoloured and still, will have a physical body with steady nerves and stable rhythm, that ails not but like a casket— beautiful yet strong as steel—serves as a "vessel meet for the Master's use," as a channel through which he can unhindered pour his blessing to the world.

Try, all of you, to cultivate a wider vision; too apt are you to over-accentuate the importance of your earth evolution. Forget not a more advanced evolution, both human and angelic, progresses on two other planets. The Brotherhood exists on all the planets throughout the scheme. Someday I will give you more light on this problem, the interest is great. But it is not of importance to you in your work now and what you can wisely use is what I seek to impart. Widen your own horizon and seek to widen that of your hearers. . . .

The petty storms and quarrels on your planet and of your cliques and groups seem serious when visioned from below; seen from above, negligible are they and of importance sufficient only to teach a needed lesson. This turmoil is but a shaking up. It serves several purposes and is being wisely guided to necessary issues:

(a) It serves to teach a lesson of tolerance and patient love. Misguided but dear to the Master are all the trouble makers, and though misplaced their energy, it is but the forerunner of a power someday to be wisely used. Give them not criticism but silence, quietness and love. Bring them each one each day in meditation to the Master, seeking to counter their distracted vibration by the Master's strong, calm and peaceful one.

(b) It serves to make men think for themselves. Anything that tends at the time to develop the mental body, especially where principles are involved, is of real value.

(c) It serves likewise to bring to an issue points that need consolidation and adjustment. This happened more previously than was intended, but all things these days are being hastened, and although it makes the strain great it brings in its train blessings of great wonder. He comes soon whom all men and angels adore.

III. The Externalisation of the Hierarchy
and the
Reappearance of the Christ

Always keep before the people the thought of the Great Ones. This is vital, and all of you must more and more concentrate on this work, the work of pre-paring the way for the coming of their feet.

The Masters are coming out among men, specifi-cally at this time among those of the western race in whom can be found vibrations analogous in some small degree to their own. A special group is forming among them now who are definitely preparing them-selves for the work of physical plane existence. Down on the astral plane are they now, hence the fact that ever more and more people are apprehensive of their presence and the utter response that comes when their names are mentioned and facts about their existence given to the exoteric students.

The three Great Ones—the Master M., the Master you love and follow, and the Master Jesus, will be especially concerned in the coming movement. Other Masters will participate too, but these three are the ones whose names and offices you must familiarise people with whenever possible. Two other Masters especially concerned with the Ceremonial Ray and whose special work it is, under the Master R. to super-vise ... Masonry (not simply Co-Masonry) will also be active in the work of the next fifteen years. Very definitely may the assurance be given that prior to the coming of the Great Lord Himself, adjustments will so be made that at the head of every great organisation will be found either a Master or an initi-ate who has taken the third initiation. ...

What is it that all of you have to do? I will enumer-ate and tabulate the matter. I give it for your wise use and it must be elaborated by yourself. What have you now? A world full of unrest, a world full of pain, sorrow and strife, a world in which the astral bodies of humanity are in a condition of tremendous disturb-ance, a world in which animals, weak women and chil-dren suffer, die and agonize, and no one cares, a world in which hunger, sin, sickness and famine, rapine and murder, stalks unarrested, a world in which the form of religion exists but the life has gone, in which science is prostituted to the ends of money, in which the produce of the earth is not for the sustenance of the race but for the nourishment of the purses of the few, a world in which good is scoffed at, self-abnegation regarded as the attribute of the fool, love itself stands for the lowest expression on the physical plane of that great force in the universe, in which all that is highest is regarded as non-essential, and all that is lowest exists for the pleasure of the masses.

Is this an atmosphere in which the Great Ones can breathe? Is this a condition in which they could find harmonising influences? Is this a state of affairs in which they could work and live? Are vibrations extant on this planet to which theirs could respond? You know it is not so, what then to do?

1. Teach the law of evolution and its inevitable corollary, perfected men.

2. Accustom the public to the thought, and teach definitely that such men exist.

3. Familiarise people with their names and attributes, with their work and purposes, and tell them that soon they come forth for the saving of the world.

4. Show that even now they are near us and teach the method of approach.

5. Breathe yourselves on every hand harmony and love. Still the violent vibrations of your environment by a strong counter vibration of love, remembering always that as you labour on the side of evolution the power of the Godhead lies with you. Naught can withstand the steady pressure of love and harmony applied long enough and steadily enough. It is not spasmodic efforts that suffice. It is the long sustained gentle pressure that eventually breaks down the separating wall.

6. (Esoteric groups) must stand for all that tends to unity. All types of work, all exterior efforts must

meet with loving cooperation and assistance. You stand in a world of endeavour, that great world that in all countries stands for the amelioration of the public hurt, as a focal point for the assistance of the Great Ones, and through you should spread forth that assistance, given in an intensified spiritual uplift to all contacts, in a firm steady stream of thought power towards the weak efforts of others, stimulating and vivifying and strengthening them, so that they achieve much beyond what they set out to do in an outpouring of financial assistance to the struggling and helpless. When you attain harmony money will come, for the Masters' work must not be hindered for need of the commodity and will not be when greater consecration and trustworthiness are found in the members. You will, if you measure up to the archetype, represent a centre of peace, power and love, practical help and spiritual uplift such as hitherto the world has not seen. Such is the hope, see you to it.

7. Definite work must be done by you in healing, exorcising, curing mental and astral diseases, and so demonstrating to the world the power that lies in the hands of those who wisely follow the Great Ones and who use this power *only* for the good of the little ones, taking no financial reward.

8. Preparation too must be done through the wise foretelling, the consecrated clairvoyance and clairaudience of your trained occultists. Much they will discern on etheric and astral levels, and when given to the scientists of the world and by them corroborated, will demonstrate to the public again the wisdom that comes to those who closely follow the Great Ones.

9. Briefly again, in legislature must esoteric groups share, training politicians and putting them when possible through fair and clean means in legislative office. No easy thing this, my brother.

10. Hospitals and schools under direct guidance of the Masters must be established. Teachers on the heal-

ing ray will come forth and wisely guide; teachers on the teaching ray will demonstrate through love and wise guidance of the concrete mind and the teaching of the pupil to hold the concrete mind in steady poise, receptive to the higher communication that the buddhic principle is the highest point for attainment now.

I have here indicated much.

───────────

Forget not that when He comes for Whom you look, He will not at first contact the world as a whole. Picture not to yourselves a sudden taking of a physical body, or of various physical bodies in various places, and a sudden plunging into the work that will attract the attention of the public, of the papers and the press. When He comes is it not more probable that (with His Masters and initiates) He will silently come, the appearing known only to the few of you in all countries who work with faithful service and unremitting zeal. I emphasise that word 'unremitting' for it holds the secret of recognition. Gathered around Him for work will be centres such as you have the possibility of forming, centres formed by the few of you who have made and kept the inner contact...who have been tried in the fire of trial and difficulty and proved trustworthy, not from brilliance of mind or achievement, but from purity of motive and the ability to stand firm.

These groups of people, having developed the capacity to work in group formation, to manipulate and carry a certain amount of power, having the faculty of the inner vision, can be led to take and carry a certain high vibration that hath a unifying and stimulating effect and enables the many to work as one. These groups will by that time have been formed in many of the great centres of life, in London, Paris, in Italy, and in America. . . . These groups will form the nucleus of the mysteries, and will be formed into various schools, recognised exoterically where definite training in the subtler bodies will be imparted to those whose vibration is sufficiently attuned to permit of admission.

One of the first things done by these groups of trained teachers will be the use of the great talismans in certain magnetic spots, and their subtler vehicles keyed up to a certain point and their lives subjected to a rigourous discipline. They will come under review by some of the great initiates who will clairvoyantly measure and register the causal body and take its rate of rhythm. If they pass this test, they will come under the direction of a very esoteric group who will prepare them for the first initiation. That will bring them under the great talisman, the rod of initiation, wielded by the Hierophant Himself. Further than this I may not bring you. I ask you but to record and watch in coming years the working out of this scheme, remembering that I but give you the outline of the plan. The measuring up to the plan lies in the hands of all of you.

Forget not that often in the past the race has failed to attain the plan, and the best has had to be made of a situation that was in many ways a failure. The hope is held in very high quarters now that this will not be so this time. It is hoped that by revealing the plan in part, and leaving it to the intuition of the people who can contact the inner side in some measure, some of the old danger of failure may somewhat be obviated. Your problem is to impart as much of this as is possible with wise choice of those to whom you give it, and share in our concern of watching the result.

IV. *The Deva Evolutions and their Interaction with the Human Kingdom*

Know you that the efficiency of a talisman largely depends upon the angel or deva that acts as its guardian? Those of you in the church who are thus linked up to the great Lord Himself, and who have these stones, are guarded by a particular angel, one of the host who are the emissaries or messengers of the Lord Maitreya. The stone acts as focussing point for His power, and is used by the angel or deva as seen fit. In moments of need, mental or otherwise, the angel of the stone—by a formula known only to him—can draw down and intensify its magnetisation for your help. . . .

In visualising the deva, you make a mental statement of the matter at issue, and ask for guidance. Then, in silent waiting, raising the consciousness as high as may be, inner conviction of the solution will gently come. Having intuitively grasped it, you may then employ the reasoning faculty and apply the solution to the matter at hand. When your intuition and your reason agree, then put in practice the advice donated.

The angel of the stone acts as intermediary, and should the matter be one that in his judgment you can adjust yourself, he passes not on the appeal to the Great One. Should it be of sufficient importance he promptly submits it.

I want to tell you something you need to remember re the deva evolution. That is, that they are on the different rays just as human beings are, and in your relationships later with them this needs to be remembered. Some are definitely on the power ray. They are the devas who are the great builders, who control all the elemental forces of nature, who are the rulers in their own realm as much as any earthly monarch. Some are on the teaching ray, and hold for your wise instruction much lore about the manipulation of the occult laws of nature, the laws that govern evolutionary progress, and closely allied with them are the devas of concrete knowledge, the fifth ray devas. These latter are paramount in importance in this five-fold evolution of ours for they go to the building of the mind. They are principally found on mental levels and wield concrete thought matter for the instruction of the masses, directing thoughtforms, sending great masses of ideas, and aiding the Hierarchy in their work of raising man from concrete to abstract mental levels, the immediate problem. The second ray devas, the great teaching of love devas, are found universally.

Devas differ from men in several ways:

The deva evolution is feminine, negative and receptive, the human evolution is masculine, positive and aggressive.

Mankind progresses through violent contact and pain; pain is caused by the positive attitude of the human hierarchy which receives and withstands the working of the Law and, in so doing, learns its manipulation.

Devas progress through acquiescence, the "going with" the Law.

Mankind learns to wield the laws because, through knowledge, they avoid subsequent pain.

Devas learn to wield the Law because they recognise its effects. They SEE.

Mankind is developing sight on all the planes; it is the inner vision, the development of the third eye, that is the goal of this manvantara, of this system.

Devas SEE, they have the intuition which is the inner sight, developed. They are on the road to develop HEARING, hence the value of ceremonial and mantric effects in contacting them. The evolution of the two runs not parallel.

Man is to develop sight, discrimination, intuition.

Devas are to develop hearing, sound, creative activity.

Man learns through pain and subsequent discrimination.

Devas learn through joy owing to clear vision, and subsequently the desire to produce the same effects they vision.

Man obeys the Law through suffering; the violation of the Law brings karma and subsequent enlightenment.

Devas obey the Law through innate obedience. They violate it not. Their problem is to copy and to build.

Humanity, at the end of the great manvantara, will have perfect vision, all will be seen and known and the Logos will have wrought out the completion of His third eye.

Devas will have perfected hearing and the sensitive ability to distinguish sound. Sound is the building force in the universe. Sight is the discriminative faculty, it deals with the choice of material; the two together will result in a wonderful coordination. With perfected vision and perfected hearing on the cosmic plane the Grand Heavenly Man will have His two head centres vibrating, and in the ensuing system comes the final third development—the will or power aspect carried to completion.

———————

Forget not that beneath the devas on the etheric planes, controlling and dominating the three dense physical levels, are other groups of entities, wrongly entitled devas, who work in obedience to the law also on the evolutionary path. You have the denser forms of gaseous life as seen in the servants of the Lord Agni, termed by you salamanders, the elementals of the fire working under them. Found are they in all that burns and in the subterranean places of the earth, in the seething bowels of the fires that in the interior of the earth live and move and work, finding vent in the volcanoes when disruptive—as often nature is— and in the warmth that holds all life in formation on the earth. Forget not, under the law of correspondences this third plane, counting upwards, manifestation of life (subtle) has its analogy on the mental plane, just as in a way little known or realised by you the first ether corresponds to the buddhic, the second to the monadic, while the atomic corresponds to the plane from whence all emanated.

Agni rules the mental plane, and has domination likewise on the third plane (or the fifth if you so term it) on all subsidiary planes. Let us get clear on this point. Always count from above; this saves confusion.

Agni, the Lord of the fifth, or mental, plane is, for this manvantara, the dominating influence, though the Lord of the fourth plane, Indra, being the Lord of the buddhic, has a subtle control that waxes ever stronger as time progresses. Toward the buddhic all strive, and in its attainment comes the system towards completion; but in the mental, or fire, plane centres the main attention of the developing system. You need to remember that just as in particular incarnations men are polarised in various bodies, sometimes the astral, sometimes the mental, so at this particular time one might infer the Logos Himself is polarised in His mental body. Towards the fourth cosmic initiation He strives. Being polarised in His mental cosmic form, He bears with Him all His body of development, including all the sons of men, as cells in that body. Hence the tremendous importance Agni, Lord of Fire, with all His deva kingdoms, on all the planes, plays at this particular time.

In an esoteric sense, all in the future becomes lighter, more rarified and etherealised; I choose my words with care. Hence, brother of mine, the importance attached to fire in this present stage of evolution. "Our God is a consuming fire," refers to this reigning Lord Agni. The devas of the Fire play an important part in earth processes. More and more power will they assume, for to them is given the work of bringing in the new age, the new world, the new continent. Varuna controlled the last transition, Agni this one. In the apparently destructive work of the fire elementals—tearing down, the burning of dwellings, and the destruction of lives, volcanic erupt ions and upheavals, earthquakes, and the blasting of great areas by fire— can be seen the constructive work of the Lord Agni, for all has a purpose. Nothing happens unwarranted.

The five great Lords of the five lower planes work in close cooperation with the great planetary Logoi. Seven there are, but only with the five connected with our evolutionary period (for ours is at this time a five-old evolution) have you anything to do just now. I give no information that is not relevant and helpful. They correspond to the head centres in the great Heavenly Men, the Lords of the seven rays and, with the corresponding human group, go to the formation of that centre. Too occult is this for you as yet. A hint of my meaning may be given when I point out to you that the head centre contains two centres, that the heart centre likewise is dual, and that the sex organs manifest a duality, though at the present stage of mankind, in separate forms. In these three you have the major centres, each dual. In the deva evolution and in the human, you have the two lines that go to the making of duality. "They without us should not be made perfect," and vice versa. More is useless as yet to impart; your comprehension suffices not.

To return to the Fire devas, of which Agni is the head and super Lord, not only does he control the fires of earth, but very definitely He is associated with the arousing of the sacred fire, kundalini. His cooperation is here needed. Now, brother of mine, note how this corresponds. I have told you before that a great part of the fifth root race (note the analogy here), three-fifths perhaps, stands close to the probationary path, and with the coming of the great Lord many

will find it possible to make the adequate extra effort
entailed in the attainment of the first initiation. They
begin to pass from the fifth to the fourth plane. The
fifth root race passes out through the fire, as did the
fourth through water, to be succeeded by the intuitional race (sixth root race) over which Indra rules.
In this passing out for this round (for the succession
holds in each round) the Lord of Fire will achieve His
particular aim for this round by the arousing of the
fire of kundalini in the large number of those who are
ready, working in direct cooperation with the great
Lord, beginning in a small way this century, and with
increased activity for the next one thousand years.

In your work, therefore, you may be shown—dependent upon your aptitude as a group to apprehend—
methods of approach to these dominating forces,
mantra that will call the lesser fire elementals, and
manipulations of heat that would be impossible without assistance. The devas of the ethers and fire elementals closely are allied, as may be demonstrated
ocularly to anyone who cares to study a flame. Note
how the orange and the violet intermingle.

All that as yet will be imparted to you has, I reiter-
ate, the specific purpose of healing. If you lose this
ideal until permission is given to investigate for other
reasons, you will arrest the teaching. In this matter
of healing and ascertaining the complexities of the
etheric body (not only of man but of much that exists),
will be varieties of information and the next step to
knowledge that awaits the race.

One final point: Each great deva Lord presides as
aforesaid over one plane, likewise over its corresponding subplane on each plane. Agni controls on the fifth
plane and the fifth subplane of each plane, always
counting from above downwards. Each deva Lord is
affiliated with one particular planetary Chohan, and
with a Chohan or Master of the humanity that has
achieved. Agni, therefore, now works in close cooper-

ation with the Logos of the fifth ray and with the Chohan of the seventh—the Master R.—who is connected with the seventh or ceremonial ray. See you the clear working out at this time? The seventh or physical plane and the seventh ray, and the fifth deva Lord and the fifth ray of the concrete mind, the scientific ray. You have there the two cycles synchronising. No flaws are ever found in the Great Law. Only your apprehension is at times faulty.

V. Symbols

The five-pointed star stands for achievement.

1. It stands for man's work and shows him what he has to dominate—through the astral, through the lower mind, through the higher mind or intellect, and through the intuition, he has to find his way back to God—a dominating of all the planes. The perfect man is he whose astral body is colourless and limpid, fit to receive impressions from high, whose lower mind responds only to the higher, whose higher intellect is but a channel for the intuition, and whose intuition is dominated by the spirit. It means that when perfection is reached and the fifth initiation taken, there is a direct unimpeded channel from the divine Monad down to the personality. As initiation after initiation is taken the channel widens. Ponder on this.

2. It stands for the five senses and their correspondences on the higher planes.

3. It stands for the fifth round, the most epochal in the great manvantara. This you cannot comprehend, except that five is the key to the mystery.

The fifth sense, the fifth principle, the fifth plane, the fifth root race, the fifth round, the fifth initiation, the fifth ray, the fifth colour of the spectrum, and the fifth cosmic plane, are closely allied. Fonder on this for it holds much. A key is here. Turn it as far as you can. The key needs dipping in the oil of the intuition. All these fifths are interlinked, and much lies in their comprehension. . . . It cannot be comprehended except by those who are ready; it serves to interest others and stimulate their thinking faculty.

More and more as the race progresses symbols will be used and words less employed. A symbol stands for a thought, an idea, and expresses in one definite form what many words would be needed to define. A symbol makes its appeal through the eye and not the ear, and directly tends to develop the intuition. First, it strengthens the imagination, that power which exists on astral levels, that world which we use to express something which is hidden from us, drawing upon our imagination for its elucidation. Then the imagination directly leads to the development of the intuition.

A symbol at present expresses four things, later it will express seven, but the future hides the other three.

1. It stands for a definite concrete thoughtform on the higher of the concrete mental levels, the fourth from the top, or the fourth from the bottom, whichever way you count it. It is the mid-most point in the education of the race.

2. It stands for a complete truth, and in its comprehension it holds the whole of evolution's story. In the mental grip of a symbolic thoughtform and its interpretation (first by use of the imagination, and later by direct intuitional insight) lies the capacity to learn and teach.

The Masters have, for the instruction of their pupils, parchments and papyrus sheets covered with symbolic designs, ranging from the simplest geometric figures to the most wonderful and intricate outlines. In these books and on these sheets are portrayed the governments of the world, the races, root-races and chains, the kingdoms of nature, the deva evolutions, the human hierarchy, and the work of all the subsidiary powers under the Logos Himself, from the great planetary Logoi and the Heads of the creative Hierarchies, through the Principalities and Powers to the humblest servant in an elemental kingdom. Each has its symbol, sign and colour, and in right comprehension lies power and capacity, lies development and evolution itself, lies the hidden wisdom and the results thereof.

Some symbols are in sealed books, holding guidance and counsel for the guides of future races and a future manvantara. All are in graded sections, and some of the simplest symbols such as the triangle, the circle, the line and euclidic designs—have been given out in ordered gradation since the coming of the Lords of the Flame.

Seven great symbols stand for each chain, for each Ray with its Logos, and for each plane and for each manvantara. The same seven describe Chain one, Ray and Logos one, Plane one, and Manvantara one, and consecutively the remainder. When the symbol that stands for these four groups—chain, ray, plane and manvantara—is known and understood, a fifth will be given. These are the seven great major symbols, numbers of lesser ones are known by disciples and given to the world holding cosmic and individual truth in each. The Masters teach by symbols and in this method lies hid the secret of the development of the intuition and the vivifying of the head centres.

3. A symbol likewise stands for an abstract conception that cannot be otherwise pictured. Some symbols stand for a concept of a truth about the physical evolution of the planet, about astral evolution (which is of greater importance) and about lower mental and concrete science. It covers truth concerning the lower planes. Other symbols convey abstract truths and cover matter that has to be *brought down* to mental levels.

Before the third initiation much symbology of the first description has to be absorbed, consciously or unconsciously; after the third initiation abstract symbols have to be consciously mastered. Definitely connected are they with the archetypal plane, and in their solution lies the power to guide in one of the three departments—governmental, religious, and natural.

4. Symbols are to be interpreted in the following ways:

(a) By their colour. The same symbol in different colours signifies different things. . . . Each ray, therefore, each plane, principle, chain, manvantara, etc., has its own colour and its own symbolic interpretation. The triangle in blue, for instance, signifies one thing, and in yellow a second, and so on, and therein lies the secret.

(b) By their position. Each parchment or book is in seven great graded sections, seven great divisions, and according to the location of the symbol so the solution. Above the line, on a line, or under a line, conveys diverse meaning.

(c) By their connection to each other. A cross with a triangle on the right teaches one thing, and vice versa another, and with all superimposed you have a third interpretation.

(d) By their key. Some parchments and books are read from left to right, from right to left, from above downwards, and from beneath upwards. This is of real interest and may be told, the four methods may be hinted at. If read from above downwards it teaches of involution; if from beneath upwards it teaches of evolution; if from right to left the history of a chain, a manvantara and root race lie hid; if from left to right the worlds in a chain, the lesser cycles and the sub-races may be seen. One page holds all four and the three that are still unrevealed.

Still another method is gradually coming forth, the sound method. It is inexplicable and unadaptable for further elucidation.

There you have the four methods, while three lie hid. Incomprehensible are they and of occult meaning, unknown even to lesser initiates.

A symbol of importance I give you:

A ball, vast as the sun, of pure white light. Across it, vertically, a Saint Andrew's Cross of blue—a blue indescribable. In the centre of the Cross, against the background of blue, a white dove, holding in its beak a flaming sword of fire. In the sphere of light around the Cross are seven balls of different colours.

Comes the interpretation: The balls signify the globes of this chain; the white sphere of light, God in manifestation; the Saint Andrew's Cross, evolution, moving towards completion, the upward arc. (The Greek Cross signifies the world at its point of involution, the crucifixion of the second Logos. In the Saint Andrew's Cross, it is the second Logos mounting towards ascension). The dove stands for peace, the goal of evolution; the sword stands for trial and strife, the method through which we attain.

VI. Discussion of: Evil : Sound : Numbers : The Sacred Word : Prophecy

The problem of evil, over which so many finite minds seek to exercise themselves, is but the Problem of contrast, the problem of opposites. Look at it this way. I am endeavouring to be simple, for what I give you I give for the sake of the little ones and few of them have minds adapted for the hair-splitting of metaphysics.

There can be no success, no victory, where naught exists to strive against; yet all is included in the One. Too much the thought exists that evil, or the power of evil, is but something with which we should have naught to do. Much you need—yes, need, brother of mine—to do with it if ever you want to know the power of good. Evil is but part of God, the power of involution, whereas you are all on the path of evolution.

Evil is, after all, if struggling men but realised it, their greatest help. It is that:

(a) By which we can distinguish light (Job 29.3).

(b) By which we get experience and the faculty to discriminate and choose.

(c) By which we develop power.

(d) Whereby we learn to see and know.

The power for evil is as much God's servant as are the forces for good. Remember you not how in your own scriptures the evil one, as you call him, has right of access to the Logos Himself at any time?

Evil is the guarantee of progress, the medium whereby evolution is possible, the great developer, the great purifier, the great educator, the great teacher. Evil and matter are but synonymous terms. Evil is the protecting shell that safeguards the delicate evolving entity.

But wisely and with judgment must this aspect of the truth be handled, for it is in its wrong apprehension that devil worship and the deification of the powers of involution can be seen. Show that matter and evil are existent only for the wise use of the evolving spirit. He passes through it and leaves it behind on his way back to God.

Evil lies in the refusal to leave behind when conquered; it consists in remaining immersed in matter that is dominated and hath no more to teach; it is the clinging to forms that should not hold the evolving spirit, in vibrating to a rhythm too heavy for the point reached; it is the holding on to things behind instead of stretching up to those ahead and before; it is a desecrating of knowledge gained and a prostituting of it to what is realised to be a retrograde and unworthy step; it is choosing to talk in the dark or twilight when just ahead the light can be seen; it is the choosing of a life of ease and no struggle, a going with the tide, when the inner voice points the way along a rocky and difficult path to a goal acknowledged to be desirable; it is acquiescence instead of aspiration, a standing still instead of going forward, a closing of the eyes instead of straining them to see a wide horizon; it is knowing and not using knowledge. The initiate James knew this when wisely he said, "To him that knows to do good and does it not, to him is sin."

Sound: The sounds of earth are increasing. The roar of the great cities, the storm of whirring machinery, the ceaseless hum that arises from the haunts of man, has a definite effect on the ethers and on all matter within the radius of its enveloping vibration. The transmutation of this sound is *the work of the immediate future*. It is the work of the next two sub races of the present root race, and of the third of the next root race. Long has this sound been in welling up and reaching its apotheosis, and long will be the process of transformation. The discord of earth has to be dissolved into harmony; the minor discordant note of evolving creation must be turned into the paeon, in the major key, of the finished system. When the final great chord sounds, struck by the Master Musician, when the seven-fold arpeggio has become the grand dominant chord and sounds forth as one sound, the effect will be to call all back again into the One, the circle of manifestation will be disrupted and pralaya will supervene.

The sound of harmony, the buddhic plane, is the plane of unity, the plane on which the at-one-ment having been made, each unit of consciousness recognises the self in all and is one with all that breathes.

Of this sound, the sound of the atmic plane, little can as yet be said, except in its connection with the mental plane. There is symbolised the cup that receives the downpour from the monad. All this information seems to you confused and difficult to grasp. So it is, and long will be, for circumscribed is the vision. A bit of information here, a little light thrown on to the subject there, a hint given on some other matter serves two purposes:

(a) It develops the intuition, gives play to the reasoning faculty.

(b) In the gradual accumulation of facts, in their wise correlation, and in general careful application, comes eventually certainty on matters as yet unknown.

Forget not, in all interpretations, in all suppositions as regards the rays, their colours, sounds, the planes, the processes of evolution, and the varying types and experiences of humanity, that certain fundamentals must be borne in mind: that this is at present a five-fold evolution. The system as a totality exists as a seven-fold evolution but, as in all else, evolution has been partial and slow. In the development of the first solar system, it was a three-fold evolution and three dimensional vision was the object attained. I told you before that SIGHT (words mislead but it suffices) is the object our Logos had in view in His three-fold system. In the first system the activity aspect was the object achieved in great measure. Now, in the development of the second solar system, the evolution is five-fold, five-dimensional vision and the five planes of human and superhuman progress. The wisdom or love aspect develops.

Let me give you some thoughts ... on the significance of numbers in the system and the creative hierarchies.

1. At each of the first three initiations (those that lead to complete control of the personality and fit the

initiate to stand before the One Initiator) comes the definite and final elimination of one of the three elementals seeking to progress through experience in the three-fold human organism. In the Bible, when you read of the great Lord casting out devils, you have symbolical teaching on this very point and a picture of the Lord initiating a disciple. You have, for instance, the man out of whom the legion of devils was cast—a man undergoing the first initiation. You have the man out of whom devils were cast which ran down a steep place into the sea. This is all a symbolic picture of the second initiation, their ejection from the mount of initiation and their re-entry into the sea of astral matter.

2. Forget not that these elemental beings themselves are progressing, and that each human organism they seek to occupy is of appropriate build. This is the obsession that is part of the logoic scheme, but which is ever *involutionary*. In the coming in of the third system these evolving elementary beings will form an integral part of the three-fold evolution of that system.

3. As before I have hinted, the Spirit of the Earth is on the downward arc of evolution, and these elementals of the physical, astral or desire, and rupa levels of the mental plane, all have their part in the building of the body of that Spirit. He is purely planetary, and each of the great planets—the seven sacred planets and the three that are hid—have each their spirit of the planet. There is apt to be confusion in the minds of the uneducated between this evolving spirit of the planet and the seven great planetary Logoi, the seven spirits before the Throne. Forget not that the planetary Logoi are evolving, while the spirits of the planet are on the involutionary path. A new term should be given to these involutionary entities. Surely planetary entities will convey a more accurate idea than planetary spirits. In the third system these

planetary entities will manifest in a strange way and form the final one of the three-fold manifestation of the Logos.

(a) *In System One* there was one dominant evolution and four minor evolutions. There were three rays in dominance, though five were in manifestation. There were five hierarchies in manifestation and seven latent.

(b) *In System Two* there are two dominant evolutions, the deva and the human. There are five rays in dominance and seven in manifestation. There are seven hierarchies in evolution, with the previous five passed on, four definitely out of range, if I may so term it, and one nearly so. The Buddha is linked to this fifth hierarchy, the final one practically liberated, hence the fact that he has passed beyond Earth reach, yet keeps his connection annually.

(c) *In System Three* will come three dominant evolutions, deva and human in dual synthesis, and the evolution — now involutionary — of the composite planetary entities. There will be seven rays in dominance at once and three rays achieved and consummated, thus making the ten rays of the three-fold system. There will be three hierarchies in manifestation, with nine passed on — seven definitely out of range, and two still holding the link. This leaves still the seven rays and the three hierarchies to make the ten to reach the goal in the system.

All this seems to you abstruse and difficult and hard to understand, yet when rightly comprehended it simplifies the conception. We look not for you to understand; much that H. P. B. gave is as yet sealed and the interpretation comes not, yet with the added elucidation offered . . . by yourself and by others who come, will light gradually break. The full dam is near at hand, the blazing out of full truth to be apprehended in this manvantara will, at the end of the fifth round, be realised though that truth will not yet be truth in manifestation objectively. By the end of the seventh round subjective manvantaric truth will be objective and consummated. The mental concept will be appreciated in the fifth round, in the sixth the concept will be brought down from mental to astral levels and there worked out, and by the seventh it will be perfected in physical plane manifestation—the physical of that period.

In the next manvantara of this system will come the working back towards unity. You will progress from the seven globes to the five, and to the three later, and eventually to the one, when will come completion of this system, remembering always that as evolution progresses will come greater rapidity of vibration and the final three manvantaras will pass more quickly than the first four, and a greater simplification will come in the system as in the manvantaras and the rounds.

Seven planets in manifestation with three hid, making the ten of this system. This is the point of greatest numerical manifestation, the correspondence in the planets of the densest point for this system. In later manvantaras will come five planets, three planets, and then one, with a period of gradual obscuration of the remaining one, for ultimate pralaya for the system is a certainty.

In the next system will come an equal proportion of simplification:

System One had ten planets in manifestation at one time, which opens vistas for your consideration, for it marked in its cycle the densest point for the system and increases the possibilities.

System Two has seven planets at its densest point and three hidden.

System Three will have five planets at its densest point, for the dual or negative-positive rays (whichever they may then be) will manifest on three of the planets, with the remaining four simultaneously on four planets, leaving one synthetic planet through which the total evolution will pass in revolution more quickly than on the other four, corresponding to the inner round of which you know nothing.

Each of the three letters of the Sacred Word has application to one of the three systems:

A, system one, wherein the first aspect demonstrated, the symbol of divine essence, the upper triangle and the formation of a basis or foundation. Incompleteness is shown in the very formation of the letter.

U, the chalice of the second system, uplifted to receive the Christ principle, the second aspect in downpouring. The chalice is formed by the activity system to be filled by the love of the second system. If rightly made, the two sides of the letter would have a termination; on the right-hand side will be found the Tau, and on the left side a lily, the Tau signifying the evolving human hierarchy, the other the deva evolution. The man forming the cross and evolving through pain, the other reflecting the attributes and learning through fragrance spent, man grasping and taking until he I earns his lesson and the devas giving and building until, through obedience and accomplishment, they arrive at the same source as a man.

M, this portrays system three, the two evolutions and the evolving third, the third lifted and aided by the other two until forced into a triangle and a resumption of the primal A without the separating bar. If portrayed in colour you could, for your wise meditation, picture the A in green, the U in blue, and the M in royal red. The colours are not the real ones but carry the hidden secret. The trident of Neptune is of great interest, it is the two sides of the chalice with the third added, the symbol at the top of the third being indicative of the third system. The A should have on its left lower arm the swastika and on the right the closed lotus. The significance is apparent.

Just a word about the evolution through pain of the human hierarchy; the devas suffer not, their rate of rhythm is steadier than the human, but nevertheless in line with the law. They learn through application and appreciation and joy in the forms built and the work achieved. Man learns through discontent and the shattering of the form. The devas build and man breaks and the same lesson of acquiescence in the will of the great One is learned.

The beauty of that will is learned by the devas through the SIGHT they have. The necessity of that will is learned by man and through HEARING the law, through the consequent breaking of that law and the succeeding pain man brings his will into line with the one Will. Devas see and learn to hear the Sacred Word. Man hears and learns to see the Sacred Word. Perfected sight, and perfected hearing, leading on to system three which adds the third quality of cosmic TOUCH, incomprehensible, but later to be understood.

Prophecy, my brother, is the capacity to—how do you term it?—surmount the various states of consciousness you entitle "time" and see all as one. As the race develops towards unity, this process of unification enters into all departments, and thus eventually becomes merged into eternity and tomorrow is as yesterday. He who has entered into the atmic consciousness sees the past, the present and the future as it concerns this greater manvantara. Such is the consciousness of the Master. He who has entered into the completed consciousness of the monad comprehends today, tomorrow and yesterday of our system. Such is the consciousness of a Chohan. But he who has in fullest degree mounted up into the consciousness of the Logos has surmounted and passed beyond the lowest cosmic plane and his conscious-ness functions on the cosmic astral, outside our solar system entirely.

Here you have the three great types of perfected comprehension or unification. In lesser degree also you find it. He who has the consciousness of the causal body has the capacity to foretell in the three lower worlds. Time for him in these worlds is transcended. You therefore frequently find people who, through karma, or attainment in past lives, in fleeting moments or through unwise methods of development can link up with the ego and read records and foresee or fore-tell. Many they are now and more and more will this be possible.

Most frequently this comes in those people whose astral vehicle is highly developed, containing much atomic subplane matter, but whose mental vehicle is weak. Being polarised high in the astral body gives them rare capacity to contact the corresponding part of the causal body. Forget not the causal body con-tains the permanent astral atom. Their clairvoyance and their clairaudience then is purely astral and not being balanced by a developed mental body leads them to misinterpretation and misapplication.

When the person is not polarised in the astral but in the mental, they can, when functioning on the subplane where the mental unit is, touch the corre-sponding part of the causal body, and then you have mental clairvoyance and clairaudience—a much more satisfactory thing. See you, therefore, brother of mine, how it goes? An astral psychic is one who in his astral body has much atomic subplane matter and can move on that subplane. He sees on astral levels, but woe-fully unreliable is he. A mental psychic is he who vibrates to the fourth subplane of the mental plane and can hear and see on these planes.

Remember above all that this is only possible in three ways, even if the matter exists in his various bodies of the needed quality:

(a) If he has in previous lives developed the faculty of inner vision.

(b) If his karma permits or if he has reached in his evolution the period when such a thing in orderly sequence arrives.

(c) If he is under guidance from a Master of the Wisdom who teaches him to break his way through the dividing web until it remains not.

The world today is in the throes of agony. Just as in the evolving ego, the moment of greatest development is the moment of greatest pain if the apprehension measures up to the opportunity, so in the evolving world. To you all who have the inner sight, the intuitive comprehension, comes the opportunity to aid that apprehension and to lead a despairing world, deep cast into the darkness and into distress, yet one step nearer to the light. The work you have all to do is to take the facts given to you by the leaders and by the Brotherhood and to adjust their application to the world's need so that rapid will be the recognition of the spoken truth.

In the heart of every man lies hid the flower of the intuition. On that you can depend, and no cosmic fact clothed in a suitable form will fail to receive its reward of recognition.

VII. *Prepare for the Future*

These are times, brother of mine, when it is the part of wisdom to look ahead, to plan, to be prepared, even to fear certain things and seek to offset them. But at this time such an attitude of mind is needless. All that comes is so uncertain that the unexpected is the most likely thing to occur, and then the force expended in undue preparedness is lost. No one can, with accuracy, foretell what will eventuate, not even those on higher planes. This for two reasons:

(a) Those who withstand us, the brothers of the dark side, are in many cases of equal power, and they guard their plans well. The end is certain, the triumph of the Light sure, but no one knows what unexpected event may suddenly occur.

(b) The, sons of men themselves react at times quite unexpectedly, and their ability to hold an attitude sustained along any line is uncertain. Even we, who see so much more clearly than you, and whose knowledge of psychology is so much more profound, cannot with certitude state just what certain groups may do. Sometimes groups with evil intent frustrate their own designs through inner defalcations. Sometimes groups that with enthusiasm pursue one line of action, suddenly change and become opposed to their own methods. This applies both to those working on our side and on the side of the dark forces.

So the part of wisdom, as before stated, is to live each day at a time, perfecting it as far as may be, dealing with each problem as it arises to the best of your ability, keeping the inner calm and the outer smile, and refusing to let the mind wander to the immediate future. The ultimate assured goal you may with confidence dwell upon, but not the foreground of the picture.

A LEARNING EXPERIENCE

by Mary Bailey

PART II—
My Story

CHAPTER 1—Long, Long Ago

These are the saddest words I know:
"Long, long ago, long ago."

I have wept for the years for ever gone.
I have mourned for the life we have known.

The careless years went, like all the rest.
Through the caring years we did our best.

But was it enough, when there's never enough—
Enough time, enough life, enough love?

There was waste; there was gain.
There was joy; there was pain.

Now the bridged heart and mind have completed
    the span.
The days and the years form an intricate plan.

The past lives today in its total effect,
The detail forgotten, a blurred retrospect.
It was so long ago, so long ago.

World War I started in 1914 when I was five years old, living in Southampton, England. I remember the terror of little understood adult conversation. I remember the fearsomely unfamiliar Yanks landing in large numbers in Southampton in their strange uniforms and boy scout hats to the tune of "The Yanks are Coming."

We flappered our way through the frivolous twenties and the thoughtless thirties, and when World War II started in 1939, I was thirty, with a seven year old daughter of my own. The years were occupied with volunteer war duties on top of my home responsibilities. We were involved in the havoc of flying bombs—the "buzz bombs," and the silent, unannounced rock-

ets. We learned to live from day to day on the sketch-
iest of rations and without much fear.

Then came my realisation that life involved so much
more than day to day survival and the everyday
events of a small family in a small world. A profound
restlessness and a deep inner discontent took hold of
me, and so my search began for a real meaning and
purpose within and behind the surface smoothness of
my pleasant, personal life.

Within a remarkably short time I came into contact with Alice Bailey's books and work, and then
realised that I needed some specific form of training.
I applied to the Arcane School in New York for information. All the work in Europe and in Britain was at
a standstill due to the war, and the English language
section of the School had been temporarily transferred
to the New York headquarters.

When I received the Entrance Papers to the School
a few weeks later, I knew I had found what I needed —
I had come home.

As soon as the war in Europe ended, Alice and Foster Bailey made plans to resume their annual sum-
mer visit to England, and came in 1947 to re-open the
British headquarters. Their house in Tunbridge Wells
(about thirty-five miles south of London), comman-
deered by the British Army for the duration of the
war, was restored to them and they returned each
year for the remainder of Alice's life to hold an Arcane
School conference and other meetings or those interested in the books and the service work.

At that time, so close to the end of her life, Alice
was seriously ill, but she made the annual trip with
Foster for those three years, including the year she
died, 1949. I met them both during those years and
heard them speak. I am glad to have known Alice even
so briefly, but my work and association has been with

Foster who took over Alice's group responsibilities at her death, as she wished and as the Tibetan confirmed.

By 1949, I was working on a part-time volunteer basis in the Tunbridge Wells headquarters. In fact, I happened to be there in December 1949 on the day the news of Alice's death arrived by cable from New York. It was an expected and a happy release for her, with her work for the Tibetan Master, Djwhal Khul, completed in the thirty years he had allowed for it. Hers was, as Foster has put it, a "triumphant incarnation." But not an easy one by any means. Any aspiring disciple can learn and profit from her indomitable spirit and invincible courage.

Alice had brought the group work to the point where, in 1949, it had spread around the world in six or seven of the main European languages. The books were not all published at that time in the English language, but the publishing programme was completed a few years later, and the translation and publication in other languages proceeded steadily until today most of the books are available in French, German, Spanish, Italian, Dutch and Greek, and several other language editions are now being added to the series; for example, the Scandinavian languages, Polish and Russian.

The books, of course, are the basis of all A.A.B.'s work, and the teachings they contain will be of fundamental importance to the externalising work of the Hierarchy until well into the twenty-first century.

Alice had also succeeded in establishing an esoteric School as a world service project, which the Hierarchy could use as needed and which had so demonstrated its service values that by the time she died it had created its own link and life-line with the spiritual Hierarchy of the planet and could, therefore, as a living organism in its own right, continue to function and expand—which indeed it has.

CHAPTER 2—Years of Crisis; Years of Change

It is a well known fact that whenever the founder of an organisation or group dies, a period of crisis or chaos usually follows. The length of time of the crisis period, and often the very survival of the work, depends upon how well the founder has prepared for the future and to what extent responsibility was already shared or delegated. Some groups never survive the ordeal, particularly where internal politics overshadow other considerations and where a power struggle weakens and debilitates the sensitive, fragile structure of a group seeking to manifest spiritual principles.

The problems can be even more acute when a *discipleship group* is involved because so very few really understand the demands and requirements of true discipleship, and even fewer are prepared to subordinate their personalities to group service. New age discipleship, the meaning and the value of group work and group training for initiation, form the significant aspects of the teaching in the Tibetan's books. He was writing for the future and for those who, as disciples, would be ready to move consciously into their hierarchical responsibilities during the final quarter of this twentieth century.

The pressures of discipleship are subtle and little understood except through personal experience. So it was that A.A.B.'s group, after her death, also experienced years of crisis and years of tension—followed eventually by an inevitable emergence. A few individuals, not willing to accept her provision for the future, left the group both in New York and in England. But others were drawn in both by the needs of the work and by their own willingness to try to function in a discipleship group. And as it has turned out, the division of the original cell has had a healthy and beneficial effect. Two or three new forms of world service work have resulted from it, and any hurt to any persons has long since been healed and resolved into good and cooperative relationships,

Foster had been so thoroughly involved with Alice from the beginning in the teaching, the books, the work of the Arcane School, and the Service Activities as they developed, that he was able to hold to a steady course, to keep the work on track according to its true destiny, and to resist many sidetracks and glamourous ideas suggested to him by others which would have jeopardised the integrity and purity of the hierarchical plan and purpose for this group organism. It was a difficult period, but also a time of learning, of stabilising and consolidation, which demonstrated the soundness and vision with which both Alice and Foster had established the work. It was a matter of uncompromising adherence to the principles on which the work was founded, and for this Foster's first ray soul was well equipped.

Crisis at the organisational level of a discipleship group usually involves two interrelated factors — money and personnel. These two factors seem to hover like the sword of Damocles, sometimes more and sometimes less apparent, but always uneasily present in the corner of one's eye — or, more accurately, as a periodic sensing of potential danger.

We have had our share of it in the Arcane School headquarters. From its inception in 1920, financing the work has always been based on spiritual law and principle. No price can be placed on the life of the soul and the spirit as it evolves its material manifestation — the personality — through a long series of incarnations. And teaching and training designed to stimulate, guide, encourage and inspire that personal evolution are similarly priceless and should be freely given. So the Arcane School training programme, all the materials and printed literature, have always been given without charge to those who need them, and distributed as widely as possible in every possible way. But since we pay rent for office space, salaries to workers, and costs of all services and materials, we have always asked that those who choose to do so should give what they can. And they always have, generously, over the years.

The only things we "sell" are the books, the *Beacon* magazine and, recently, the video-tape recordings of meetings and interview programmes. These group activities involve the purchase of special materials, and printer's costs, which are too much for us to bear without a guaranteed return.

We have learned through the years that the spiritual law works—when we let it. "Those who live by the law must abide by the law," it is said, and where financial resources are concerned this is an infallible essential. One does the work, unfolds its programmes and activities and plans for future development and expansion without necessarily having any money available in hand to do it, but with the utmost conviction that need must be met and as the work is done it will magnetically attract all needed resources. There must be no fear, no hesitation, or lack of faith, although faith, in time, must be superseded by the conviction of knowledge and experience.

If the work is in line with the Plan of Hierarchy, and if it is wisely and intelligently planned and executed and all possible steps taken to give form to vision and idea, the money *does* flow. The key words are "Having done all, stand." This is the *occult* technique of energy flow—"energy follows and conforms itself to thought "—and not the mystical notion that "the Lord will provide" so long as one is good and kind and doing so-called "spiritual" work. The occult technique, which is the method of Hierarchy, views money as the densest and most material form of energy—which is essentially divine—a form which has become so tainted and imprisoned by human greed and selfish desire and so locked up in cornered markets which benefit the few to the detriment of the many, that its release into rightful function and right relationship with the spirit or life aspect of energy, requires an identical release in those who work occultly to give money energy right direction. The occult disciple has bridged, or is in process of bridging, the gaps in his own consciousness which seem to separate spirit from matter. Heart and mind, love and intelligence, work together in him under the impression of the spiritual will to contribute to the planetary bridging process whereby, eventually, Hierarchy and humanity will fuse into a single centre of energy, so bringing closer to realisation the logoic goal of a perfectly manifested relationship between spirit and matter.

The mystical attitude is "let go and let God." The occult attitude is "hold on and help God." *Physical manifestation* of the fifth kingdom, the kingdom of God, the soul, the Christ principle, is the purpose of this second solar system, and that requires the active cooperation of all forms of conscious life on this planet.

The occult process must be consciously adopted by those who seek to release money energy for hierarchical work. And there's the rub! The attitude is too often more mystical than occult, more trusting than knowledgeable, more resigned than resolved And spiritual growth cannot be forced by outside forces; it can only respond to inner recognitions and pressures, although the Hierarchy itself, the Masters, can and do apply pressure if they deem it useful and wise and likely to hasten the soul's progress in monopolising its personality vehicles. And the consistently right use of money energy demands a high standard of discipleship and soul fusion.

There are, and have always been, periods of intense financial difficulty in this group, when the bottom of the barrel has been nearly scraped through and one needs the skill and manipulation of a juggler to keep all the associated activities alive and active. This was always Foster's responsibility while Alice was alive, and it has been mine also for many, many years. Lack of such a fundamental and vital ingredient as money draws on the spiritual integrity of an individual and a group, and can sap the energy of the workers and distort vision if the attitudes are incorrect or the resolve weakens. "The crux of the work problem is a financial one," the Tibetan has said, and "you are called upon to solve it."

Solution always depends on the quality, the integrity and the spiritual standing of the group personnel. So both these factors, money and personnel, contributed to the crisis years that followed Alice's death.

A group, like an individual, is always in process of becoming. One never arrives, one is always in transit, although there are recognisable stages of growth and, in the earlier phases of spiritual unfoldment, there are periodic plateaus, places of pause, consolidation and reflection. But these disappear as consciousness expands and vision and revelation succeed one another more rapidly and consistently. "There is always a new world in process of becoming," we are told; the further one sees, the more there is to see.

Group members stand at many different stages on the path, linked together in service by love of the work and the soul's inclination. But sometimes differences can arise at the outer level of the work and its activities and within the personalities of the workers which may supersede the inner strength of commitment and love. When this happens there can be change and movement in personnel.

There is also the fact that not all who try the experiment of group work and group training are necessarily soul-directed. There can be what the Tibetan Master calls "spiritual selfishness" both in motive and in performance, but there are many reasons for personnel change. For example, some serve in the group for a limited period of time only—long or short—leaving eventually to go on to some other experimental effort which may be more appropriate for them. It is not always apparent to everyone what is the right place of service until experience itself clarifies and directs.

A group, and the disciples working in it, should always be prepared for personnel change, and for personal change if necessary in the best interests of the work, but the soul's intention and the needs of hierarchical work should be the determining factors and every faculty bent towards making those recognitions which will equip one for a more adequate contribution to group good, group goals and group integrity. And progress is slow until the individual centre of attention shifts from the self to the work. This is a major step forward because, whether recognised and admitted or not, every aspiring disciple during the early and intermediate stages of growth is profoundly concerned with his own ideas and opinions and deeply interested in his own actions and reactions. He has not yet "lost himself in order to find him-Self." Or, as Foster used to say, when the disciple can reverse his preoccupation from "*I am* serving the work, to *the work* is being served," then a basic transformation has taken place.

For several years following Alice's death there was some change and movement in the personnel of the headquarters group—in New York, in England and in Europe.

About 1955 or 1956, a new headquarters was opened in Geneva, Switzerland, to serve the students working in five or six languages in different countries. This meant a shaking up of the old arrangement and of workers in several different countries. In 1960, the

British headquarters was moved from Tunbridge Wells to London. It was realised that we needed to be more accessible and to have a closer contact with other serving and special groups if the Service Activities were to develop as they should. We occupied offices at two or three different localities before finally settling (in 1978) in an ideal area close to the Parliament buildings and all other governmental agencies. In Geneva, we were fortunate to find space in a new building near the Palais des Nations, a building sponsored by the Swiss government and maintained as an international centre for service oriented organisations.

In New York also, we moved in 1965 to a new building near the United Nations where we seemed, again, to be in our right environment as a worldwide service group. This has served us well for twenty years, but, as I write this, a move is underway to new premises. For one thing we have outgrown our space in the United Nations Plaza and need room to expand and, for another, a renewal of our lease would have brought an impossibly heavy increase in rent.

The move in London to offices in Whitehall Court is an example of the way money flows to meet a need when the attitudes are right, the vision clear, and the planning intelligent. In Whitehall Court It was required that we purchase the lease on our office space, a matter of a very large sum of money. At precisely the right time we became the recipients of two legacies and a special gift totalling more than 113,000 pounds, which provided for the purchase and the additional structural costs. This is a fifty-year lease in a government protected building—an historical landmark—so we are set for the immediate future without rent to pay but with a monthly maintenance charge and what the British call "rates," that is, in the U.S.A., "real estate taxes."

I suppose the nub of all this is that one should always be prepared for change and should not be discouraged or dismayed by it. In fact, Alice used to say that if nothing is happening in your life, make it happen! Constructive change is a part of growth, and even where reasons and trends are not clear at first, it is essential to make the best and the most of the opportunities change presents, for indeed "obstacles (or crises) are opportunities!" Sometimes one can turn a potentially harmful or negative situation into positive channels because at the heart, or root, of every negative force lies the germ or seed of a positive energy.

CHAPTER 3 — Foster Bailey

In her *Unfinished Autobiography*, Alice Bailey writes at some length of the part Foster played in her life and her work, and of her abiding gratitude and appreciation for him. "He made my work possible," she says. If this were true of the thirty years they worked together, it is even more true of the years after her death when Foster had to assume the major responsibility for making sure that the work continued according to plan and to its basic hierarchical principles, and that it continued to expand in scope and in usefulness.

I feel, therefore, that I cannot go any further without speaking of Foster from my own intimate knowledge of him during the twenty-seven or so years we worked together. Because of the very closeness of our relationship, I have hesitated to write about him, and indeed I find it difficult to do so because so much must be left unsaid.

Foster mentions in his article "The Discipleship of Alice Bailey," which forms the introductory chapter to this book, that he and I had the identical ray energies throughout all our vehicles from the soul ray to the physical. While this was so clearly true, we were nevertheless very different people, due to the other influences that create the finished product of a personality, and our "human relationship" required just as careful attention and nurturing as any other, particularly in the earlier years. But from the beginning we both knew, and gloried and marvelled in the fact that essentially ours was the continuation in this life of an old and ongoing relationship rooted in the ashram and intended for the development of the ashramic work in which we were both involved. And, as Foster remarks in his article, quoting Djwhal Khul, when this meeting of two people with identical ray equipment occurs, "it is impossible to keep two such people apart in their discipleship work."

At the time of Alice's death, Foster was in a seriously depleted physical condition. The long years of strain and effort in caring for a very sick Alice and in doing the work with her and for her, had taken their toll on an already tired and weakened heart. He fully expected to follow Alice quickly. But it became immediately apparent that his presence was needed for some time in the work itself to stabilise and bring the group through the crisis years without compromising its basic principles. He spent some time at the old victorian house in Tunbridge Wells (England) during 1950, '51 and '52, working in the large garden and resting in the sun. It was during this time that he and I came together in recognition of shared work and of a past—and future—relationship emerging once more in the present for certain specific purposes.

Early in 1952, it was found that the head of the British work at the Tunbridge Wells headquarters had developed terminal cancer and had only a few months to live. I remember writing Foster a note telling him that "until he could make other arrangements" I could give some more time to the work at headquarters—"I was available." That resulted, not in a little more temporary help, as I expected, but by being thrown head first into the deep end on a sink or swim basis! And I remember remarking to Foster one day that surely I needed more training for what I could then dimly see lay ahead of me. His response was merely, "The work itself will train you." And I have often recalled the Tibetan's comments, "You learn to work by working," and "You will learn from your mistakes, my brother." Certainly I made mistakes, many of them, from which I hope I learned enough to go on each time for another stretch of the road. One of Foster's favourite maxims used to be, "Let me not pass this way in vain; let me not make the same stupid mistakes over and over again."

Looking back, I realise again how much I learned from Foster, without actually being taught. He had an endless store of stories, anecdotes, jokes, rhymes and ditties, going back to his youth, which came out at both appropriate and inappropriate times, causing me amusement often and irritation sometimes. I have never known him to be at a loss for words. He was a great talker and would have made a good trial attorney if he had continued in his law practice.

But essentially, Foster's distinctive characteristic was his discipleship and his total dedication to discipleship work, non-fanatical, quiet, humourous, but intense. He did what had to be done, no matter who or what was involved. This sometimes created the impression of ruthlessness, and he earned an unjustified reputation at one stage for over-forcefulness and a disregard of people and their feelings. Actually, he was a loving, compassionate, tender and acutely sensitive man. He could not have done his work successfully for Alice, and later, without that combination of firmness and sweetness.

Although he was loquacious and detailed in conversation, with his fourth-ray mind examining every facet of a topic or problem, in his writings and public speaking, Foster was always precise and sparing. He never equivocated; a spade was a spade to him or, in today's idiom he "told it like it is." World affairs were his favourite topics, and the working out of hierarchical plans for humanity his constant preoccupation.

Perspective and proportion are needed by a disciple in balancing the responsibilities of discipleship with the duties and obligations of a normal daily life. But Foster had little patience with aspirants so wrapped up in their own personality lives and so fascinated by their own doings and thoughts and feelings, that the discipleship aspects became of secondary importance. "A little discipleship as convenient," he called this, and of such a personality preoccupation he used to say, "Nothing matters very much, and most things not at all."

I learned one invaluable lesson from Foster very early in our association. He always did what he thought was right in the light of "God's Plan for man," as he called it, and lived through the consequences without reaction to the opinions or reactions of others. In his own words, "Do what you have to do, as wisely as possible, and then let the chips fall where they may." "Don't react," he used to say to me, "live above it, let it flow past you." In the sort of life both he and I had to live for the work and with the group, this was an essential attitude to live by. Praise and blame, commendation and criticisms, have come our way, to Foster as they did to Alice, and to me, and we have had to remain unaffected by either.

Through the early years of our work together we did a fair amount of travelling, speaking with groups and in public and meeting students and others. But after about 1962, shortly after our marriage, Foster's health condition was such that he could no longer stand the strain. After that I travelled alone, and in my various journeying to different parts of the world so many people have spoken to me of their love for Foster and their appreciation for his contribution to Alice's work. When I passed these messages on to Foster, he was genuinely astonished. He could never understand how anyone could love him!

I think perhaps that the greatest accomplishment Foster made in his own personal discipleship was the ability to subordinate his strong and definite personality to the work and wishes of another. To work successfully with Alice, he had to put his own thoughts, opinions and preferences aside and carry out what she, in her discipleship commitment, wanted done. The teaching came through Alice because of her readiness to function in such a direct and responsible hierarchical relationship, and Foster recognised the importance of her work and deferred to her in everything that pertained to their work. This must have been difficult; to stand behind and to support someone else no matter what was involved, and to be willing to become, as Foster did, "the Mr. Bailey of the Mrs. Bailey!" demanded humility, clarity of vision and a true sense of "the fitness of things."

For the last ten or twelve years of Foster's life he was confined entirely to our Manhattan apartment as a semi-invalid— with an occasional emergency trip to the hospital. His office days were over, but his work went on. In those last years he built up a correspondence with individuals in different parts of the world whom he recognised as "thought leaders." Most of these were active in the educational field, which was of first importance to him, but many served in the political, religious or philosophical worlds. Foster always looked for the real values in what these people were saying and doing, and then he would write them, not seeking to teach or inform, but expressing appreciation for what they themselves were contributing to the upliftment of the human race and the world as a whole. He always evoked a fascinating response, and built up a useful and interesting correspondence with many who came also to appreciate the values they found in him, as their letters testify.

Foster's overriding wish during his life was "to be useful" and this he fulfilled right up to the time of his death. He was born in Massachusetts during the famous blizzard of 1888. All his life he was a rebel, unconventional, a non-conformist, sweetly unreasonable at times but always unutterably sweet, a true disciple in the purest human and hierarchical sense— the Masters have no space for "yes men." He died peacefully early in the morning of a clear, summery day on June 3rd, 1977.

CHAPTER 4—Discipleship

Basic to all aspects of the Ageless Wisdom teaching, and to all concepts of service, lies the common denominator of discipleship. It is stated in the Master D.K.'s teachings that while there are three major phases of the Path of Return and three major aspects of discipleship, everyone—"from the humblest aspirant first setting his feet on the Path, up to and including the Christ himself"—is a disciple and should not make any other claims either for himself or for others.

The three stages of the Path of Return are: (1) the Probationary Path; (2) the Path of Discipleship; and (3) the Path of Initiation up to, and including, the completion of the fifth initiation which transforms the fourth degree Adept into the "Master," a fully integrated member of the spiritual Hierarchy, the fifth planetary kingdom. Therefore the three stages of discipleship are: (1) the aspirant or probationer; (2) the disciple; and (3) the initiate.

There are, of course, many variations and lesser stages within both of these classifications, but while detail and circumstance can vary greatly and the sub-stages proliferate, the Path of Return must be trodden "in the full light of day," that is, in full consciousness. It is the Path itself which provides the graded and sequential opportunities for all disciples because the Path is woven out of the redeemed substance of our own consciousness. Covering so vast a span of evolution one would think that "discipleship" should be a relatively easy idea to understand and practice—since it is the way we must go—but the reverse seems to be the case.

The word "disciple" derives from a Latin root which has been interpreted to mean a pupil, or a student, one who learns under the tutelage of others. But while treading the Path of Return is certainly a learning experience, the more accurate interpretation is, "one capable of applying the necessary *self-discipline* to the personal self," which will eventually dissolve the many mental, emotional and physical barriers to self-knowledge. Nothing can be accomplished—by an aspirant, by a disciple, or by an initiate—until he "knows himself" to be what he has always been in essence, an embodied fragment of divinity, destined to reveal that reality in daily life as a conscious contribution to the planetary logoic goal of reconciling spirit and matter.

In the early stages, therefore, discipleship is concerned with self-recognition, until the personality does indeed become a clear lens through which the light of the soul may irradiate the environment. In the later stages the emphasis shifts, first to the effort to manifest the idea of service—a basic soul and discipleship principle—into ever larger and more inclusive spheres of influence, and later to the realisation that conscious cooperation with planetary evolution is the destiny of the fourth and fifth kingdoms—humanity and the spiritual Hierarchy, working together. All else then falls below the level of consciousness, including the need for self-discipline and the compulsion to love and to serve, for these have become an automatic way of life and no disciple/initiate of such a degree could function in any other way.

The details and requirements for discipleship in its many phases are set out clearly, in detail, and in the context of the various forms of relationship in which we, on this planet, are involved, in the many books A.A.B. produced with and for the Master Djwhal Khul. They have been, they are today, and they will be in the future, a source of inspiration and encouragement to many. But in my own experience during these years I have found that while many accept what they think the teaching means by discipleship—some with devotion and an element of fanaticism—comparatively few are willing to accept the self-discipline aspects of discipleship or to *change*, utterly, their own cherished or preconceived ideas, opinions, feelings and reactions. And. change is what true discipleship demands, a demand made not by any outside source or any body of teaching, or by any "Master" or guru, but by the true inner self, the soul or Christ principle. Such a demand is made when the time has come for a drastic reversal and reorientation of the personality way of life. The *soul knows* when the time is right, the soul can be trusted; the soul demands and the shrinking personality must, sooner or later, respond.

One of the barriers to a fuller and more adequate response to the soul lies in the over activity of the concrete mind. A would-be disciple can long, ardently, to become the serving soul, a true disciple, and seriously try, and believe, that the necessary changes are taking place; and yet the bias, the rationalisations of the mind, and the longings of the desire nature, set up a deceptive fog of illusion and glamour in which the purity and simplicity of the soul's nature and the reality of service become blurred and distorted. And with this fog of illusion a sort of complacency sets in which causes the cutting edge of the sacrificial will-to-be to blunt and slow down. I have seen this so often. If the soul could only answer the plaintive cry of the personality, "I am doing all I can," it would undoubtedly say, "Not by a long shot!"

On the other hand, I have known many disciples in all parts of the world, and worked with many on a day-by-day basis, whose selfless dedication to the work of Hierarchy and to the Christ demonstrates their discipleship status without need for words. I would say that in the course of the last fifty years the numbers of those self-directed into discipleship from the depths of their own conscious experience in "living the life" of the soul have more than quadrupled. Every one of them, and many more besides, are needed by those who seek to guide and direct the Plan for humanity through this critical period of the twentieth century, linking the old age of Pisces with the in-coming age of Aquarius. Many, many more now engaged in the effort to achieve real discipleship—to "become the Path"—will move rapidly ahead once they are determined, and have learned to let go of their personality preoccupations in exchange for something greater, wider, more illumined and illuminating, more joyous, and more useful to the Hierarchy.

All the many experiences of daily life, whatever they may be for any individual, help to prepare him for discipleship and infusion by the soul; but there is nothing comparable to the discipleship condition and nothing that can ease the way or really modify the exacting standards and qualifications required in those who will come into relationship with the members of an ashram, and with the greater Ashram itself, the Hierarchy. The risks of admitting the unprepared— the incompletely transcended personal self—into such an area of responsibility are too great, both to the ashram and to the aspiring disciple, and the Masters too wise and experienced to risk disruption. But they do take risks when the odds seem to warrant it, and they do know that every young disciple newly absorbed into an ashram can, and usually does, cause a temporary problem which the ashram as a whole can neutralise. The Masters also submit an "almost disciple" to a forcing process which will speed up the process of soul-infusion by facing the individual with vital and difficult choices. The result is always indicative of the actual status of the disciple.

It is always good to remember that while the metamorphosis from aspirant to disciple to initiate proceeds, the inevitable accompanying struggle and pain —mental, emotional and physical—is temporary and entirely personality centred. As the disciplined personality transforms and transcends its own limitations, suffering decreases to be replaced by a suffusing joy, a radiating love, and a newly enforced spiritual will. Truly "only the personality suffers; the soul knows no pain." What a relief, what a release, to have put all this behind one, to have learned the needed lessons, and to be free to direct one's whole attention and all one's energy resources to the accepted service, whatever it may be.

It is hard for the young disciple, even the most fiercely independent, to realise that all this growth, however long it takes, is a matter of one's own intention, one's own effort and initiative. The teaching which shows us the way to go cannot do it for us. Each person is unique and must experience the way for himself, making his own mistakes and interpreting the word symbols in the light of his own experience as he goes along. This was part of the teaching of the Lord Buddha also, as it is of all really spiritual leaders. The Buddha said, in effect, "Hold fast to *the truth* as a lamp. Rely on yourself alone; look not for help to anyone outside yourself." And according to the Christian teaching, "the kingdom of heaven is within you." And there lies the way of the disciple, the answer to all questions, and the resolution of all problems.

I was reminded of this while listening to the CBS "Sunday Morning" programme on October 20th (1985). There was an appreciation of Ansel Adams concluding with a small part of a rare interview he gave not long before he died. Speaking of his work and the mystical and magical effects his camera recorded, he said, in answer to a question (and quoting someone else) "If you have to ask, 'What is it?', you're never going to know!"

The spiritual progress of a disciple is made more difficult by the paradoxes and apparent contradictions of the Path. What is right at one stage is wrong at another (which gives us the clue to the problem of good and evil) and what is right for one person may be quite wrong for another. It is also necessary to bear in mind the endless variations and qualifications one must apply in seeking to understand and benefit accordingly. There are no rigid compartments or divisions or clear, single definitions one can use as answers and explanations. So there is an outstanding need for tolerance, for the ability to see and accept things and people as they are and not as we wish they were, or think they are. We have to learn to "change the things we *can* change," which means in ourselves. Two people of more or less the same spiritual standing can see the same events in two totally different lights and, unless there is a genuinely achieved degree of soul control, the results can be damaging to a relationship.

I remember being uncomfortably present during a heated and hurtful exchange between two people, both of whom could see only their own right and the other's wrong, whereas in reality both were right and both were wrong. Finally it was suggested that perhaps it would be in order to "forgive and forget," whereas one remarked, "I can forgive, but I can't forget," surely a contradiction in terms for the words are synonymous!

To me, that is an illuminating and typical example of a stumbling block on the Path of Discipleship all of us encounter and all must surmount. A disciple, in process of becoming an initiate, must let go completely of personality hang-ups, personal hurts and reactions, which prevent progress and impede others as well as ourselves; for our negative thoughts and broodings and all unresolved personal tensions are out of line with the evolutionary current; they infect the atmosphere and the fall-out affects our whole environment. When personal matters are involved, it is easy to forget that we are a small part of a larger whole. It is for the benefit of the whole that we expand our consciousness and purify the personality, and to the detriment of the whole when we fail to do so. In the words of the Agni Yoga teaching, "Attain and conquer. You do not conquer for yourself alone."

So the negativities and the personality reactions must be "let go" to lie behind in our past experience, to become part of the way we have travelled, contributing to growth and experience, but belonging to the past for which there should be "no recollection."

Simple? Yes. Easy? No! But essential.

CHAPTER 5—Group Work in a Discipleship Perspective

We know that while in the past the very few disciples available have been individually trained and prepared for initiation, today, as we enter into the age of Aquarius, the training is provided in group formation. Group initiation will increasingly become the hierarchical method of the future.

This idea is a new and difficult one to understand accurately. Many today misinterpret the concept and oversimplify its meaning due to the intellectualism of the concrete mind which has no precedent against which to measure and evaluate the new requirements of the in-coming age. These new methods will also become exoteric to a degree with the externalisation of many esoteric principles and forms of teaching, and this too will create its own new and unique problems.

The Arcane School group was set up as "an experiment in group endeavour," and while mistakes have been made in the process of learning and experiencing, much has also been gained over the years. A certain degree of group consciousness has been developed and enough understanding of the idea in its new age setting to establish a good foundation for the growing demand for a more adequate manifestation of its realities.

As with all forms of esoteric teaching, we are expected to take the principles and the concepts involved, interpret them for ourselves, and then subject our understanding to the acid test of "learning by doing." New age group work is, in reality, the outer manifestation of an inner and genuine spiritual condition, and a testimony to the conscious ashramic relationship developed slowly, and often painfully, over many years.

Group work is not, after all, a totally unfamiliar concept. In fact, 500 years before the work of the Christ in Palestine, Gautama Buddha established his work in India through small group communities set up to be self-supporting and interdependent, each within itself and all in relation with one another. The Buddha saw this method as preparing for an eventual "world community." Today, 2500 years later, the need for a global consciousness and an interrelated world of nations—a world community—is recognised as imperative to the very survival of the planet. We have become *interdependent* in so many areas of human life, but not as yet properly *interrelated*. Yet there is a common denominator—relationship.

Whenever I think of this, I am amazed at the long-range vision and planning, of the infinite patience of those who stand in the forefront of planetary evolution. May it ever be so, for the human family, which occupies a key position in the planetary life linking the subhuman with the superhuman kingdoms and acting as a planetary transforming centre, is erratically wayward, wilful and unpredictable. The God-given gift of freewill is still bogged down in its self-will aspect, a long way from the joy of surrender. This is a condition which is likely to continue for many millennia as the slow process of transformation and transfiguration gradually produces its illuminating effects.

The seed of the new age group idea, having been sown long ago, is now due to emerge recognisably in all parts of the world. It is today, and will be in the future, interpreted and practised in different ways at varied levels of consciousness. So far as the new age teaching is concerned there are two major aspects of group work which should be recognised. One is the type of work to be adopted by groups of men and women of goodwill. And the other is the type of work to be developed by disciples.

Both types are needed and each needs to be understood in the context of its own accepted responsibilities. Both are still in the experimental stages of growth through experience, the discipleship requirements necessarily being far more difficult to understand and to practise, because largely unfamiliar hierarchical vision and methods form the framework of such groups, rather than the accepted and familiar norms of the society in which the groups of men and women of goodwill serve.

The Tibetan Master, Djwhal Khul, made the attempt during Alice Bailey's period of work with him to teach and train an outer, esoteric group of *disciples*, seeking to establish such a standard of unified group endeavour under soul control that the preparatory training for group initiation could be accepted. He failed in this, or rather the group he had in training failed to accept the needed rigourous training in personality transcendence and subordination to group good. But the record of the work done, as recorded in Vols. I and II of *Discipleship in the New Age*, is illuminating and of infinite value to those consciously approaching the same goals.

The essential differences between serving groups of men and women of goodwill and groups of disciples consciously cooperating with the process of planetary evolution, seems to be this. Men and women of goodwill come together as an outer consequence of the cosmic *Law of Attraction*. That is, they meet and know one another as more or less dedicated and selfless personalities, sharing a similar vision and compatible, as personalities, in their ideas of service and the ways and means of making a group contribution to meeting human need. With occasional exceptions, there is liking, respect and loyalty between the group members and a willingness to work out differences and compromise on methods.

On the other hand, a group of disciples (evolving eventually into a "group disciple") is first of all a subjective formation influenced by the cosmic *Law of Synthesis*, forming a centre of soul consciousness responsible, under ashramic influence, for working out on the physical plane a definite part of the great Plan of Hierarchy for humanity. Everything such a group undertakes fits into the ashramic purpose and is influenced by ashramic need.

In such a group the work itself, the Plan, is the magnetic force attracting and synthesising the personalities in service, and all else becomes subordinated to this paramount need. The personalities involved frequently may not meet or know one another or, if they do combine in outer groups, may not necessarily like one another. Compatible personalities are seen as irrelevant to a central group purpose wholly concerned with some aspect of hierarchical work. There is, as the Master D.K. puts it, "neither liking nor disliking, neither approval nor disapproval, neither criticism nor non-criticism" within a discipleship group. He says, "Where there is liking, then too strong a personality relation is established, as far as the good of the group is concerned. The group equilibrium is disturbed. Where there is disliking, the inner faculty of *rebuff* works constantly and cleavages then occur." (*The Rays and the Initiations*, 209).

What actually exists in a true discipleship group is "a real comprehension of 'divine indifference,' spiritual detachment, and deep, persistent, unchanging love," because such a rare group, when it exists, "is brought together under karmic law, ashramic necessity and soul direction. . . . There is little to link these people except inclination, a joint aspiration and a goal seen and held in unison." (*Ibid.*, 210). The relation between such group personnel should be, as D.K. mentions in one of the D.I.N.A. books, "friendship in its purest sense," that is, friendship as the Hierarchy knows it, impersonal, unfettered and totally supportive of Plan-directed work.

These are intensely difficult ideals to translate into practice. Few can struggle through the pain, the petty personality reactions and resentments, that fog the clarity of soul direction and ashramic intent. So the personnel of outer discipleship groups tends to change from time to time, more today than it one day will when the pull of the ashramic work proves stronger than the reactions of a hurt or frustrated individual. New Age groups, in common with all other varieties, are as fragile or as resilient as the weakest links or units within them.

We have seen many changes in the Arcane School headquarters group over the years, and no doubt will experience more in the future because we are involved in a *process*, a pioneering process which all disciples must work out for themselves at their own pace, in their own way. The actual and central configuration of a group disciple, formed under the Law of Synthesis to help "create unity" at the outer level of human affairs and human relationships, is the compelling energy within the whole process and the guarantee of continued growth along the hard "way of becoming." The first ray fuels the urge-to-good and the tenacious drive forward.

A disciple in a group schools himself, trains himself, prepares himself, contributes his own efforts and his own being to the group whole, and does so voluntarily, without coercion or any outside pressure. His subordination to the soul principle—in himself, in the group, and in humanity—and to the purposes of the ashram—responsible for group plan and purpose, is the result of his own choice and willing cooperation. And this is eloquent of the changing emphasis in new age discipleship groups. As distinct from the old-age established method, Aquarian-type groups form not around a central and controlling person (not even the Master) but around a central and controlling purpose or idea. This represents the purpose of the ashram, a recognition of that aspect of the Plan of Hierarchy for which the group can rightfully accept responsibility. This is primary; it motivates, inspires and propels into action. Its magnetic and radiatory force creates and sustains the channel of communication between the ashram and the outer group; and that channel must be presented intact if the group is to provide the expected and needed cooperation in externalising, or "making manifest," ashramic ideas and ideals.

Although the central, magnetic motive in such a new age group is the *work*, unitedly visioned and organised, there is also a central point of responsibility in every discipleship group. Alice Bailey once said in an address, "At the centre of every group stands a world disciple," a disciple whose experience and utter self-forgetfulness provide the means whereby such a responsibility can be safely exercised, with self-effacement and without any taint of personality authoritarianism.

Djwhal Khul gives us the correct pattern which an outer group, linked with the Hierarchy, must adopt for safe and accurate energy communication. He points out that members in such a group are not identical in spiritual unfoldment and experience or in ray relationships. They stand at various points on the path of return and are linked at the soul level with various ray ashrams. This provides the breadth and outreach the group needs and, in D.K.'s words, "a wide field of relationships." In addition to the central point of energy responsible for maintaining the free flow of energy from the ashram, there are two others with a special link and function within the group, the three forming a central and essential triangle which then interacts fully with all other parts of the group structure, creating a network of energy communication from the centre to the periphery and from the periphery to the centre.

The words used to describe such an essential group pattern may be relatively easy to understand intellectually, but to experience the condition itself in operation, to feel and know it in heart and in mind, and to provide the fullest possible cooperation with the smooth functioning of the whole group as one link in "the chain of Hierarchy," is another matter altogether. Few—even with the best of intentions and purest of motives—can live up to the ideal. Personalities, and personality differences, too often interfere with the selflessness needed, for right attitudes leading to right actions are often too fragile to sustain under pressure.

I have seen so much of this over the years, and so much unnecessary pain and disruption, due to inability to *live the teaching* and to *practise the principles* of hierarchical work. And yet, it is all a matter of actual spiritual growth. When it comes to a working cooperation with the ashram, one cannot pretend, or assume, or claim a degree of spirituality not actually attained. The reality of the status of a disciple always reveals itself through the way the work is done, through the way relationships are handled, through the priorities and the reactions in day-to-day life, and the way the individual responds to pressures and problems, in the work and in daily group contacts.

As the new age unfolds and the energy of Aquarius acquires more influence over the way humanity thinks and feels and acts, disciples too should find it possible to swing the balance of their own lives more fully into the soul centre and the ashram where service of the Plan, based on love of humanity, is a natural and perfected way of life.

CHAPTER 6—Claim-making

It is a fundamental and well-known principle that no one of any genuine spiritual status ever resorts to claim-making. This isn't so much a matter of careful self-discipline or watchfulness, but of an actual self-forgetfulness. Spiritually evolved and responsible individuals are so indifferent to their own status—and to that of others—that it forms no part of their day-to-day thoughts and activities. If the matter does arise, it is in relation to some essential purpose or event, or person, which may be temporarily relevant to an ongoing service project, or to a significant relationship.

One of the seven Principles of the Arcane School states: "No claim is ever made . . ." either for the School or for those who serve at headquarters. Those who study the teaching and seek to live it in daily life can use this principle, not only as a guide for personal attitudes and behaviour, but also as a scale on which others may, if necessary, be weighed. Discrimination in the evaluation of people, as well as events, is an important element in the exercise of, and the ability to, choose and decide wisely. To repeat an earlier statement, one may claim to be a "disciple," since the road of discipleship extends from the lowliest neophyte to the Christ himself, but no true disciple of any degree of initiation would proclaim his actual position on that path.

Yet, in spite of this, many today are publicly claiming their own advanced spiritual degree and, in many cases, that of others. And in doing so, reveal only the inaccuracy of their perceptions and the glamour of their conclusions. These exaggerated claims may often be made for reasons of personal prestige and the desire to control and direct persons or activities which seem important to them. In fact, self-importance is usually the outstanding characteristic of claim-makers, particularly in those cases where the claimant tries to convince others that he, or she, is acting under the direct instruction of one of the Masters of the Wisdom, or of the Christ, who want this, that, or the other done.

I have seen so much of this in my work with the Lucis Trust and the Arcane School. Even while Alice Bailey was still alive she was contacted by various individuals who claimed that "Master D.K." wanted them to correct various mistakes made in his work with her. After she died the numbers increased, particularly in the effort to change the wording of the Great Invocation. In recent years, several have claimed to be the "successor" to Alice and to be receiving the new teaching from the Master, in spite of his own words concerning the next, and final, phase of his teaching.

It is useful to note that the Tibetan himself was fully aware of the potential dangers inherent in producing teachings emanating from a Master of the Wisdom within the Hierarchy. It is a highly glamourous situation, fraught with pitfalls for an incompletely transmuted personality. In the effort to offset the dangers as much as possible, D.K., in *The Externalisation of the Hierarchy*, talks about the "thoughtforms of the Masters" existing on the astral plane and created by the devotion, desires and emotional misconceptions of aspirants and devotees. These thoughtforms are potently energised and well organised by those who create them and are, therefore, drawn to them, insubstantial as they are as total misrepresentations of the Masters who are completely disassociated from them.

It is these "astral shells", these deceptive thoughtforms that many contact and mistake for the reality, although it is almost impossible to convince anyone personally influenced by them. The general attitude is "others may be deceived by these thoughtforms, but not me!"

In recent years, and as the Christ and the Hierarchy draw nearer to humanity, the glamours and illusions have extended to the person of the Christ also. So many today in different parts of the world claim to be the "second coming," that if any one of them would only apply even a little intelligence and common sense, they would realise how ludicrous and impossible such claims are.

Yet they continue, sometimes quickly fading away into obscurity and sometimes attracting a good deal of attention and support. A few years ago I was approached by one of these so-called "Christs" who demanded that I turn over the Arcane School to him since he needed it as a medium for his new message. When I ignored the demand, I was angrily informed that I would be "removed by death," and he would then take full control of all D.K.'s work. A few weeks later the poor deluded man, trying to prove to his followers that he was "indestructible," jumped from a high-rise building in New York and suffered the inevitable consequences.

Attitudes behind these exaggerated claims can vary considerably. Some are exploiters and manipulators for personal ends; some are genuinely self-deluded; and some are simply ignorant or naïve. A few years ago in Australia I met one of the latter variety, a young man who introduced himself to me as "Sanat Kumara." He was puzzled and bewildered by the fact that no-one would accept him, or correspond with him, by that name. I tried to tell him that he obviously did not understand the identity of Sanat Kumara, because if he did he would know that he could not possibly claim that identity. His reply was, "I read that Sanat Kumara is also known as 'the eternal youth,' and since I have discovered the secret of eternal youth I *must* be Sanat Kumara!"

It is more difficult to respond to the sincerely deluded than to the charlatans and power seekers. But, in living the esoteric life, spiritual integrity demands a strict adherence to principle, although there are some circumstances when a "little white lie" can do more good than harm in bridging between the credulous or impossible and the reality of spiritual truth. It was a basic injunction of the Lord Buddha that we "hold fast to the truth as a lamp, for all else is ephemeral and withers away." Sometimes it is difficult to distinguish between the true and the appearance of truth, and it is in making these distinctions and learning to discriminate using the touchstone of *principle*, that understanding deepens, consciousness expands, and light increases.

In the hurly-burly of daily life in which all disciples are involved in one way or another, we make our way by evaluating and choosing, balancing the pairs of opposites so long as the personality fluctuates between the extremes of good and evil, and learning the values of compromise and adjustment in the interests of an overall goal and purpose. But such adjustments can affect only the means we use to achieve a clearly visioned spiritual goal. "Never compromise a principle," is sound advice, but we need also to recognise that there are greater and lesser principles and the lesser can always be sacrificed to the greater. A closed mind or rigid attitudes, even when based on a true idea, reveal the grasp of a partial truth only. The real seeker after truth is flexible in attitude, willing to consider aspects of a truth which have so far escaped notice, and aware of the fact that there is no finality to truth. No one can claim a finality or perfection in the approach to truth, or to the divinity which we all imperfectly represent.

The question arises as to the best way to cope with the claims of those who persist in trying to force them on others, with the many who see themselves as the chosen "messengers" of the Masters, and with the effort to authenticate "instructions" from a Master affecting the work of a group such as ours. It has been our general practice to ignore such claims and efforts on the principle that, by responding to them or paying attention, or seeking to correct mistaken ideas, one is simply increasing the problem by giving it the energy of thought and attention. The biblical injunction, which the Tibetan Master also emphasises, of "resist not evil, but support the good," is sound advice. Energy does "follow and conform itself to thought," and the less attention paid to false claims, messages and instructions, the sooner the glamour and illusion may dissipate, setting free the unfortunate victims of self-deception.

Sometimes, for the protection of the work, it has been necessary to register an initial rejection of the claim made. In such a case, the rejection should be clear and unequivocal, made without rancour or ill-will and released as soon as made; that is, put out of mind from that moment on, so minimising possible repercussions or reactions either of one's own or from the source of the problem. One has to be prepared also to have one's own rejection rejected, either angrily or sorrowfully, and without any further responses. It is a well-known truism that we cannot convince by argument," therefore, it is better not to argue.

By and large, the claims of the ignorant or the self-important do little harm to the work of the Hierarchy. They can be irritating and exasperating; they can cause some would-be disciples to hesitate or turn aside into a *cul-de-sac* for a long or short period of time, while the learning process goes on. To experience untruth, or so-called "evil," for oneself is to recognise eventually that indeed "good is best," and there is no teacher like personal experience.

The work of the spiritual Hierarchy led by the Christ is well established, so much so that the externalisation process is well advanced, and this demands so much attention and energy from all disciples that the lesser problems and delays which inevitably accompany the path of evolution, can safely be left to the passage of time and the process of growth.

CHAPTER 7 — The Reappearance of the Christ

It is impossible to think, or write, or participate in this group work without realising that the Hierarchical reason behind it all is preparatory for the reappearance of the Christ. This is a matter of timing, of evolution, of the evocative condition of human consciousness, and the unfoldment of planetary and systemic history according to Plan.

We human beings inevitably tend to evaluate cosmic events in terms of our own narrow and circumscribed horizons. It is because of *us*, we think, for *us*, and with our consent and cooperation that inner causes work out in outer effects in our familiar world and immediate surroundings. And certainly little could be done without a sufficiently ready condition in human consciousness as a whole, and without enough intelligent, willing, and selfless disciples and cooperators. But the motivation behind the fact of the Christ's imminent reappearance lies in the evolutionary circumstances and needs of the solar system and its Informing Life, of which our planet is an integral part. Long cycles of time and zodiacal eras combine together to produce events and opportunities which, if rightly interpreted and used, create conditions appropriate to the birth and growth of new states of consciousness—human and solar—and expansions of understanding. Such a condition exists today and in a unique and portentous form.

It seems that we are not only entering a 2,500-year cycle of Aquarius (the personality cycle) but also the larger 25,000-year cycle (the soul cycle), and we are also about half way through the process of a major transference on the wheel of the greater zodiac of 250,000-year cycles. These transition periods cover five thousand years, and the process into the influence of Aquarius on the greater zodiac began with the coming in of the Piscean era 2,500 years ago. These great cycles represent the monadic cycle. Such an alignment within the energy influence of Aquarius will have tremendous repercussions which, today, we cannot possibly visualise and all forms of life will be drastically and permanently affected.

The energy and significance of the Christ—the "Son" at-one with the "Father,"—is of vital importance to the opportunities for a new synthesis and at-one-ment, vertical and horizontal, provided by the influence of Aquarius. And in today's psychologically and spiritually divided world where everything *physical* tends to coalesce and unite for the common good, the opportunity as well as the need for a genuine unity among the cultures, religions and races of the world was never more urgent.

The Christ, having achieved his cosmic identity with Life, or God, carries that piercing, fusing, all-inclusive force which fires and inspires, which fuses and opens out, every state of consciousness sufficiently open and receptive to be transformed. Only the Christ, to date, has achieved such a condition from the purely human state of being. Only the Christ, "the first in a great company of brothers," can use this Aquarian opportunity for cosmic purposes and for human development together and in an interrelated sense. The times are indeed unique; the Christ is unique in his own stage of development; the opportunity is unique.

It is little wonder, therefore, that the Hierarchy has made, and is making, an all-out effort to stimulate spiritual growth in those associated with the ashram, literally "forcing" growth in those they can influence and holding open the channel by which "the call of Hierarchy" sounds out constantly and continuously. The Hierarchy today is concerned only with the task of preparing for the Christ's return, and with the need for many members of the Hierarchy to precede him and to come with him. All the teaching and training provided in many different forms is directed to that end, because humanity in general cannot be pressured or forced into a new age of changed energy influences and greater spiritual maturity. There must be willingness, cooperation, and a sustained and selfless drive forward based on an understanding interpretation of the ways and means offered or suggested to us. We can be shown the way, we can be taught the techniques and the need for change, but no one can do the work for us, although we are just as responsible for the right timing of planetary evolution as are those whose consciousness is already "full of light" and far deeper and more responsible than our own. The Christ and the Hierarchy cannot do it all without us, so that, in a very real sense, humanity is also today in a unique situation. We have never before in history been capable of such a degree of conscious cooperation with a Plan far more comprehensive and inclusive than our limited minds can envisage.

So the Christ's reappearance is a deeply esoteric event as well as a most practical necessity at this stage in history when all planes of consciousness must be—and can be—involved together in spiritual movement. The physical plane is the place of manifestation, and it is the *manifestation of the "Kingdom of God"* to which all growth is now directed. Therefore, the need for a second physical appearance by the Christ, the God in man, who spearheads the whole process of entry into the Aquarian experience.

Alice Bailey's books are full of comment and new thought on the reappearance of the Christ, particularly in the book of that name and in *The Externalisation of the Hierarchy*. It is clear from the teaching that the subtle levels of human consciousness—the mental and the emotional—are already affected by the potency of the approaching Hierarchy, led by the Christ. Two phases in the process of the reappearance, and the first to occur, are the awakening of the Christ principle in the human heart, affecting the emotional nature, and a mental response affecting sensitivity to impression. But this factor of a stimulated heart and mind is creating a good deal of unfortunate, but unavoidable, glamour and illusion. Energy, impersonal in itself, stimulates whatever may be present in a person, a group, or a nation, whether positive or negative, good or bad. The potency the Christ carries needs our adjustment and understanding response. We have to condition ourselves to its powerful stimulation if the results in consciousness and in action are to be positive and therefore of service to the whole process of the reappearance. It is the over-stimulation of a state of mind already prone to illusions and glamours which has caused, and is causing, so much trouble for the Hierarchy and so many claim-making and misleading fanatics within humanity.

While only the rare occultist can glimpse something of the cosmic dimensions and implications of that unique event we call the reappearance of the Christ, millions of people the world over, of all races and religious beliefs, expect and prepare for that second coming in their own terms. Buddhists expect the coming of the Maitreya Buddha, the Supreme Buddha; Mohammedans, the Imam Mahdi; Jews, the Messiah, and so on. The work of preparation takes certain quite specific forms. There must be a real measure of peace and unity among the peoples of the world, and this again depends on specifics; peace and unity are the consequence of right human relationships and human rights accepted, respected, and observed everywhere. This is the sequence: goodwill, leading to right human relationships, leading to peace on earth, and the emergence of the Christ with his Hierarchy, leading to "glory to God."

With the climaxing experiences of the Piscean age and the impact of the incoming energy of Aquarius, a tremendous stimulation is affecting all aspects of human nature. The good and the bad, the material and the spiritual, are rising to the surface of life in confrontation and conflict, clearly visible for all to see. The old fights to maintain its supremacy, and the new creates opportunities and possibilities which many today vision and strive for. When a real balance is struck between these conflicting forces, and the human mind responds to new thinking with acceptance and the joy of discovery, the way into the future will clear sufficiently and the Christ and his associates can safely complete the process of externalisation on to the physical plane without risk of over-stimulation or of the imposition on humanity of a way of thinking and a way of life other than by conscious choice and decision. Humanity is capable of right thought, right choice, and a right solution to world problems of our own making, and we are responsible for making that choice.

The Christ has a new message to bring to Aquarian humanity and a new teaching to give. These will be adapted through whatever form of life and field of service he chooses to adopt, whether it be political, educational, religious, scientific, or whatever. The place, the means he will choose, have not yet been determined by him, or if they now have, are not known as yet to the world's disciples. There is still much to be done, subjectively and objectively, mentally and physically, through an all-out effort by those who have accepted some responsibility for the work of preparation.

According to the Master Djwhal Khul, the Christ will appear wherever the most effective preparation has been made, creating conditions compatible with the energy the Christ will bring. D.K. tells us that the work of preparation is our "first and foremost duty," and that the most important part of this is "teaching people on a large scale to use the Great Invocation."

In all the Lucis Trust work I have known for the past forty years, the Great Invocation has played a central role, because it "embodies the complete new utterance of the Christ" and is, therefore, our main instrument in preparing for his return. As one examines the Invocation in this context it is clear that we need a much deeper and more inclusive understanding of the three basic energies the Invocation presents, because they, in turn, embody the significance of the Christ's work throughout the Aquarian era.

What *is* Light, as the Invocation expresses it? What is Love; what is Power? It seems that the Christ will *manifest* a new facet, or aspect, of these basic cosmic forces as his work unfolds throughout the coming centuries. Therefore, today, perhaps we should strive to slough off the complexities and complications introduced into modern human and international relationships and seek solutions to world, national and more personal problems within the simplicity of the basic energy foundations on which God "created the world and all that is within it." Light and Love and the Power of the Will-to-Good are pure and direct forces which can, if we use them, clear the way into the future by establishing mutual trust, cooperation, and understanding relationships on all levels in all areas of human life. These energies have been made available to us *for use* and it is only through using them that we shall familiarise ourselves with their qualities and meaning and open up a whole new world of energies and forces.

Today it is thrilling to know that from the first early efforts to translate and distribute the Great Invocation—forty years ago—the work has spread around the globe and broadened out into the modern communications media of radio, video, and television. In the course of my work and travels, I have heard the Invocation voiced by small and large groups in their own languages, a moving experience. I remember one occasion in Cape Town (South Africa) when a large group of performing dancers and singers, and as a special gift to me, sounded the Invocation in their Xhosa language. This took place in the open air after the performance, under the star-bright southern sky, in the shadow of the mountains. The group itself was hidden by the curtains separating the changing and make-up areas from the stage. Only the voices could be heard, like a single chanting voice, rising and falling in the cadences of this exotic language. It was an unforgettable experience.

Into remote parts of the world the Invocation has penetrated, its origins unknown for the most part, but the words, and the meaning of its own special non-verbal language, clear and dear to those who use it and respond to its potency. So many have said to me in surprise and pleasure, "Oh, *you* use the Invocation too" which always makes me smile.

Thinking of the function of the Great Invocation in the future, we can only come back to the words, "The Great Invocation is the complete new utterance of the Christ." It is, then, obviously up to those who use and work with it to discover what makes it "complete" and why it is "new." And one can only find the answers in the energy components of the Invocation. Energy is in constant movement, therefore, in constant change. This makes it particularly difficult for the finite human mind to pinpoint and stabilise a meaning and significance at any moment in time. But it can be done by drawing parallels and analogies, from the known to the unknown, from the infinitesimally small to the infinitely great, and also, as the esotericist is taught to evaluate, "from the universal to the particular."

As we move into this most significant Aquarian epoch, we must be on the verge of new discoveries concerning the construction and use of Light and Love and Power. In these discoveries, science has a major

part to play and a definite responsibility to bridge
still further the already narrowing gap between science and religion, science and politics, and science
and the social areas of human life, all of which have
been so seriously eroded with the passing out of the
Piscean era largely dominated by the sixth ray energy.
A new world—which means a new humanity—is at
the birthing hour, and the Great Invocation is a major
instrument made available to the growing numbers
of Aquarian midwives.

As the Master D.K. has clearly pointed out, when
the cosmic, planetary and human heart centres have
been brought into alignment through the realistic use
of Light and the radiation of Love, motivated by the
Will-to-Good, then the Christ will come and nothing
can stop him. Under Law, he will be "pulled through
into expression" by the inevitable consequences of the
magnetic and radiatory condition within the planet.
The physical plane of the fourth, the human kingdom, will then become his immediate field of service.

CHAPTER 8—Many Are Called

Evolution may seem to be slow, but what incredibly different conditions exist today at the second coming of the Christ than during his period of work in Palestine. Then he could select only twelve apostles, or disciples, to help him in his work. Today, hundreds of thousands, probably millions if the truth be known, have been called to his service, and most of this new possibility seems to have emerged during the course of this century. Foster always called these potential servers "Christ's own people," and hoped he could be numbered among them.

The Master D.K. has said that it is only since the year 1900—the beginning of the twentieth century—that humanity has been capable of providing any significant cooperation with the spiritual events initiated by the Hierarchy, such as the Wesak Festival, although obviously much growth has been germinating unseen and unknown below the surface of 20 centuries in time.

Nevertheless we still see even today that while "many are called, few are chosen." And there may be several reasons for this. For one thing, the Hierarchy and the Christ have spread their net and sounded their call to service far and wide. Hitherto closed doors have been opened—by the Hierarchy because of humanity's own persistent and insistent demands—and opportunities are extended through that radiation which stimulates and evokes response. According to D.K. humanity has surprised the Hierarchy by an unexpected readiness to accept responsibility more than 2,000 years ahead of time and to proceed into new states of consciousness and areas of service. This readiness is apparently not a matter of any one or two specific parts of the world or types of humanity,

but is a pervasive and widespread condition, infiltrat-
ing and permeating human consciousness as a whole.
Such a condition provides the foundation for solid
new growth, and acts as a leavening agent affecting
all and everything. Therefore, the "call" today is to
the many.

That "few are chosen" must be viewed in a compar-
ative and proportionate sense. The reason for it lies
in the hierarchical method of extending opportunity
through "forcing" the energy of goodwill—love—into
the human centre, and sowing the seed of spiritual
principle and value broadcast to allow for both the
"good' and the "stony" ground. The inevitable weaknesses, the unevenness and lack of balance in humanity, automatically eliminate or screen out the unready,
those whose personalities are not yet sufficiently purified or transformed to permit of a safe contact with
the tremendous potency of the fifth kingdom in nature.
At the same time, wherever there is even a chance that
light might penetrate and enliven, the opportunity is
provided. And "stony" ground may not continue permanently in such an arid condition. Persistent tilling
and fertilising can produce extraordinary effects, and
the prepared ground of a human mind and heart will
receive, nurture and eventually germinate the im-
planted seeds.

There are glamours surrounding this hierarchical
work in which so many are involved. The call of Hierarchy is profoundly stimulating, and where a true
humility does not exist as "an adjusted sense of right
proportion"—as D.K. defines humility—personalities
can become inflated with self-importance and a sense
of "apartness," the chosen few, the Hitler or Nazi complex. The true disciple, with the need and the call of
Hierarchy sounding permanently and silently within
him, does not see himself as "special," he does not
separate himself from the human race, or stand aloof
in criticism and condemnation. He is *human*, he exists

to serve humanity, his service consists of the energies he transmits in his daily life through his own being aligned with the source of Being, translated into attitudes and actions appropriate to his particular skills and aptitudes and training. He essentially serves through radiation, which implies a closely meshed relationship with the great network of human hearts and minds and with the planetary "chain" which includes all life within the planet.

The Master Djwhal Khul has asked us specifically whether we understand the significant value of "service through radiation." A selfless response to the call of Hierarchy opens the energy centres, brings them into alignment and right relationship, and permits the life force to flow out, through the aura, in a free and unimpeded way.

The "chosen few" can therefore be identified today, not in racial, religious, group or national terms, but by the *quality* of the life lived. All who serve the Christ and the Hierarchy are fallible, subject to failures of performance and judgment. Most still struggle with some form of personal weakness or glamour, but the overall quality and effect of the life lived serves some specific need or some aspect of the emerging Plan which is of far greater importance than any surviving personality faults. *Using* the "talents" we have instead of bemoaning their meagreness, increases their value and leads eventually to a transcendence of personal hindrances. We remember the parable of the buried talent which failed to increase, buried through fear and a sense of impotence.

There is no ultimate, there is no finality, to the energies we receive in the intention to be of service — to the Plan, to the Christ and to humanity. We resolve to follow the Christ's example; we place ourselves in that position which can best produce the needed results and changes in ourselves; and gradually the alignments are created, the relationships are established, the channel of living energy communication begins to open and clear itself of impediments, energies flowing more fully and freely the more the instrument of the daily life is used in service.

The prayer of all true disciples is "to be more useful" in the great planetary scheme of things. Usefulness increases as the disciple becomes increasingly absorbed in service to the Plan, increasingly drawn into the stream of the Christ's work, increasingly capable of usefulness and usableness to those whose "call" has drawn out his response and the best he has to offer.

CHAPTER 9—Conclusion

As I have spent time preparing and writing this material, I have found that practically everything I expected to do with it has changed, including the title. Originally I had thought of the title *Looking Back*, over the more than forty years I have been associated with the science of esotericism and with this work, including thirty-three of them at headquarters. The writing I have done myself seems to have had a mind of its own, and as different aspects and phases of the work came up in my mind, it was not so much the sequence of unfolding events and happenings but with a realisation of how much I have learned from it all and how privileged I have been to have had this opportunity. So I am calling this book—if it should eventually become one—*A Learning Experience*. I also know well that others involved in the teaching of the Ageless Wisdom cannot help but learn, much or little, depending on the individual.

It has always been significant to me that the esoteric teachings provided by various members of the spiritual Hierarchy are intended more for the expansion of consciousness than for the acquisition of knowledge. That knowledge *is* acquired is important of course, but relatively incidental. That consciousness should expand is vital, or whatever knowledge may be gained cannot be fully and accurately used as a service tool.

An expanding consciousness is a broad and inclusive consciousness, a more synthesised state of awareness in which the units and parts of a whole are seen and understood in relationship—part with whole and whole with part. And since a basic objective of the present and the new incoming cycle is to establish right relationships and create unity, an ability to relate both knowledge and consciousness, intellect and intuition, to this objective automatically expands the concept of *service*, the be-all and end-all of it all. The recognised environment of one's life expands at the same time, extending in ever-widening circles—outward, inward and upward. We are here to serve the purposes of the Creator for His creation, and esoteric teachings should be an invaluable tool in the process.

But here too there is an important lesson to be learned. The teaching provides techniques and tools, but the wielding of those tools is a matter of personal interpretation and application which, in turn, depend on dedication to service and the discipleship capacity to work as the Hierarchy works, and to "keep on keeping on" no matter at what cost or disruption to the personal life, or what the discouragements and obstacles.

In the context of the teaching, I have come to understand something of what the Master D.K. means when he says that there are two kinds of disciples in the world, "the conscious and the unconscious" and that the "unconscious" disciple can frequently provide more useful opportunities for hierarchical work than do those conscious of what they see as their "special" status as disciples. It all boils down to the real purpose behind the teachings. Since they are not primarily intended for the acquisition of knowledge, there is only one way that an expanded consciousness infallibly manifests its presence to the Hierarchy and that is the ability to *practice the principles* of the Ageless Wisdom. Where the fundamental meaning and the basic spiritual principles within the informing Life of this planet are in process of practical application—manifestation—through any one or any group, the teachings based on these principles are not always necessary, although those who accept esoteric teaching and training can acquire a plus factor, an added faculty, in their service equipment. But the meaning and purpose of it all is *manifestation*, manifestation of the soul, the Christ principle, the "Kingdom of Heaven This is *living* the life as distinct from the critical analysis of a technique or teaching, or acquiring tantalising intellectual tidbits of information. Djwhal Khul has said that probably the greatest sin of all is to know and not to do.

As a tool and as a technique, the teaching, once absorbed, can sooner or later be relegated to the background, which may sound shocking or heretical! But we cannot forever lean on and rely on *techniques* of service no matter how fascinating, how true, and how useful. Consciousness must expand beyond the need to lean and to be propped up or reassured on anything or by anybody.

The teaching the Hierarchy has given us, is giving us, and will continue to give us in the future, is true, needed, factual and inspiring. It should not be discarded or relegated to inconsequence, but it must be seen for what it is and used for confirmation and documentation when needed. A disciple should realise that the fusion of his consciousness with that of the fifth kingdom, the spiritual Hierarchy of the planet, is a basic objective of the teaching and when that happens, or is in process of happening, it supersedes, while it includes, all the effort and the experimentation that have led up to it. From the point of view of consciousness, no part of the teaching is discarded, none of it is irrelevant, but its essence and its purposes are built into the outgoing capacity to serve. That open link with the Hierarchy, once established, is never lost. It forms the central core of a disciple's life, always available, always accurate, always reliable.

According to the *Agni Yoga* (Roerich) teachings, the Teaching should always be revered, even above the Teacher. And indeed there is reverence in the gratitude one feels for the tools we have been given in the teaching and the sacrificial efforts of those who have undertaken to equip humanity with the means of lifting itself up by its own bootstraps, and of taking its destined place within the planetary Life as a cooperator and co-creator with God. "Thy Kingdom come; Thy Will be done, on earth as it is in heaven" means manifestation, the physical emergence of spiritual reality. "Let Light and Love and Power restore the Plan on earth" means the same thing. The "centre which we call the race of men" is the place where material forces and forms and spiritual purposes and energies come together in a visible and recognisable fusion for the benefit of planetary evolution, which includes all kingdoms, and to the "glory of God." This is the *raison d'être* of the teaching.

So far as training schools and groups, like the Arcane School, are concerned, these will continue for a long time to serve a useful and indispensable hierarchical purpose. There is need in the world for such schools. The teaching needs to be assembled in logical order and sequence, organised into progressive stages and presented to those who seek training in a form they can adopt, or adapt, to personal need. It is well known that the Arcane School is based on three basic requirements—study, meditation and service. *Study*, in order to grasp the principles and propositions of the Ageless Wisdom in their modern form for Aquarian disciples; *meditation*, to acquire the only means whereby the link in consciousness can be created with the central life force informing the superhuman, the human, and the subhuman kingdoms. Again, meditation is a technique, a means to an end, and there are many different and effective techniques taught by a variety of groups and teachers. The *way* any of these techniques are actually used in the practice of meditation is a highly personal and individual matter, however. And it has always seemed to me that there are probably as many ways of meditating as there are meditators.

Essentially meditation, like a study of the teachings, is intended as a service and to increase the capacity to serve, until it becomes truly planetary and of usefulness to planetary evolution. Meditation, no longer a technique, becomes a way of life, a state, a condition, a projection of the soul which is in "constant meditation."

The third basic requirement in the Arcane School is *service*. There is nothing new in the concept of service. Two thousand years ago the Christ taught that to love and to serve are the characteristics of a good and truly "spiritual" person. My own definition in this day and age when we are all becoming so much more aware of the truth in the occult aphorism that "all is energy," is this: *Service is the right use of energy to meet a recognised need on any level of consciousness.* And that includes all aspects of life, material and spiritual, objective and subjective. Effective service can be a subjective, silent, concentrated and sustained use of energy, selected, appropriated and accurately directed according to the perceived need. This can parallel, replace, or precede a physical activity, the two together including both the inner causes and the outer effects of some condition.

Service should not be confused with "do-gooder" attitudes, although many, but not all, of these more obvious and visible types of service do provide help and are evidence of good intentions and a compassionate attitude. "Do-gooders" are frequently open to criticism because their actions are not always particularly intelligent or discriminating and are seldom based on a knowledge and consideration of all aspects of a problem. Sometimes one must "be cruel to be kind," when those to be helped are refusing to face reality and the truth that practically all our personal problems are self-made, due to our inability or refusal to face the need for change in ourselves.

Change and growth, movement and expansion, inclusiveness and loving understanding, these form the building blocks that we ourselves create and build into the "yellow brick road" of the path of evolution. This is the path of the antahkarana, that bridge in consciousness which spans the gap between the Life force informing every atom of substance within the planet and its actual 'real-isation', or duplication, in the way we consciously choose to live our daily lives as liberated human beings on the physical plane. This is the meaning of that occult phrase, "Before one can *tread* the Path one must *become* the Path." Or, in my own words, *the Antahkarana. the Path, is woven out of the redeemed substance of our own consciousness.*

This is a basic objective of the Arcane School, the real esoteric work, which is offered to students to do with as best they can. Again, the School can only show the way, suggest a technique, and the student must do the rest. In my opinion, the Arcane School does this better than any other esoteric school I have known in the course of my association with the teaching. Alice's genius established the basic principles and major structure of the School from the time of its inception, and although much of the training program itself has changed over the years—which it must—the sound, essential structure has been meticulously maintained, simply because "it works!"

I have been associated with so many wonderful co-workers at the three headquarters centres—New York, Geneva and London —whose inspiration and initiative have supported the work, strengthened its link with the Hierarchy and offered a usable channel to the Masters of the Wisdom and the Christ. And I have known and worked with hundreds of dedicated individuals and groups around the world whose work in the place where they are is acting as a needed leaven and lifting agent in the stupendous task of helping to establish right human relationships.

I cannot sufficiently express my love and gratitude to all these men and women, whose group sense and self-forgetfulness are opening out a deeper meaning to the reality of the Aquarian consciousness. Some time in the future we shall be brought together again to work, as a worldwide group, for the new principles the Christ is preparing to establish when he comes.

A LEARNING EXPERIENCE

by Mary Bailey

PART III—
A Sampling From The Past

CHAPTER 1—The Principle of Freedom*

In these days of an almost universal acceptance of the principle that "all men (and nations) should be free" to decide and work out their own destiny, it may be difficult to realise that the urge to freedom has been a motivating impulse dictating the behaviour of masses of peoples for century upon century. Freedom, as we now understand it, has only recently been accepted as a normal, natural *right* to be expected, to be enjoyed, and to fight for if denied. Franklin Delano Roosevelt summed up the basic freedoms in his four brief statements: Freedom of speech and expression; freedom to worship God; freedom from want; freedom from fear—"everywhere in the world."

Within those four freedoms, as they struggle for universal application, many others are coming to the surface of human life to receive attention and action from those directly affected by them. The many well known 'liberation' movements fall within this category: 'black' liberation, 'women's' liberation, the liberation movements initiated by politically (and economically) oppressed peoples living under various forms of government, and so-called 'freedom fighters'. The central urge towards freedom is present within all of them, although motives are frequently mixed and the factors of power and profit taint the philosophical purity of many who distort the ideal by violent, often criminal, methods.

To avoid trapping and limiting the ideal of freedom by the pitfalls inherent in human fallibility, there are two related principles to be kept in mind. One is the

---

* Editorial in the November/December 1983 issue of *The Beacon* magazine, Lucis Publishing Co.

sense of universality—knowledge of human unity, the oneness of all life, and respect for its preservation and integrity. This would prevent claimed freedoms from becoming a license to do as one pleases regardless of the rights, the wishes and the welfare of others and of other forms of planetary life. And the other, is the simultaneous development of a sense of responsibility.

Many years ago Queen Juliana of the Netherlands included a potent little phrase in one of her public speeches, "Freedom," she said, "brings its own responsibilities." Since then, many others have used the same words and sought to reveal their true meaning through responsible action for human welfare. Indeed, one can easily see today from many examples throughout the world, that a claimed freedom within any area of human life, if selfishly or materialistically exploited, produces anarchy, disruption, and increased suffering for countless people, many of them innocent victims of the circumstances of their birth.

To be consciously and constructively applied within some area of human life in the world, the principle of freedom is therefore indissolubly allied with a sense of responsibility and a perception of the universality of all life. These are the fundamental spiritual values which motivate the activities of members of the new group of world servers.

Behind this spiritual freedom and substanding the principle of freedom, lies an aspect of the Law of Evolution, with which esotericists will be familiar, the Law of Freedom, a cosmic Law which has been focussed as a divine principle through the sun Sirius into direct contact with our planet, Earth. This mysterious relationship and some of its effects are described briefly in *The Rays and the Initiations*, pp. 416-7. We are told: "The principle of freedom is a leavening energy which can permeate substance in a unique manner; this divine principle represents an aspect of the influence which Sirius exerts on our solar system and particularly on our planet. This principle of freedom is one of the attributes of Deity (like will, love and mind) of which humanity knows as yet little. The freedom for which men fight is one of the lowest aspects of this cosmic freedom, which is related to certain great evolutionary developments that enable the life or spirit aspect to free itself from the impact, the contact and the influence of substance. . . . (the principle of freedom) is that which 'substands' or lies under or behind all progress."

From these words it is apparent that the urge to freedom is an inherent part of the substance of the vehicles used by every soul in incarnation. It has been a slowly developing, slowly emerging force within the evolutionary process for aeons of time; necessarily slow, so that a sense of universality and a developed sense of responsibility could simultaneously unfold to ensure the correct use of the Law for the benefit of the whole human race. What we are witnessing in the world today, therefore, is more a climaxing emergence in line with the Plan than a spectacular and often destructive force wielded in desperation or under some subversive influence. The destructive or negative aspect of any new influence always, we are told, emerges first; to be followed, as responsible servers take hold of the principles to be manifested, by the positive and creative aspects.

These are recognitions we all need as we struggle through the climaxing crises at the end of the Piscean era and prepare for the new dispensation of the Christ.

CHAPTER 2—Establishing Right Human Relationships*

> The fate of men and nations is determined by the values which govern their decisions.

If there were such improbable beings as "visitors from outer space," and if they had the facility ascribed to them by some of their proponents, of understanding the language of anyone with whom they happened to come in contact, I would guarantee that any of them picking up a daily newspaper in almost any part of the world would be baffled and bewildered!

The news these days is full of contradictions. On the one hand, news of actual wars, violent revolutions, war counsels—thinly described as departments of defense—and the production and widespread sale of horrendous, sophisticated, thermonuclear weapons, fills pages of every paper and every news report we hear on radio and television. On the other hand, reports of "peace" efforts abound—in the United Nations and outside its jurisdiction, and increasingly news is mounting from around the world of organised, interactive groups working for peace, many of them these days originating among professional groups—doctors, lawyers, scientists, the churches, musicians, authors, and today, even within the ranks of military personnel, both active and retired. It's a widespread demand from every element of human society. And these groups are increasingly international; for example, there is the group called "Scientists for Nuclear

---

* Address given at a public meeting in Stockholm, Sweden, October 5, 1982, titled in Stockholm: "Mankind's Future and the Need of Right Relations between Individuals and Nations."

Disarmament," and a group called "Physicians for Social Responsibility." I heard a Canadian speak recently at a conference I attended at the United Nations, and he made the comment that many doctors are becoming members of this particular group, "Physicians for Social Responsibility." It's a rapidly expanding movement. And there is "International Physicians for the Prevention of Nuclear War." The two founders of this international organisation are, one, the American, Dr. Lown, and the other, a Russian, no less a person than Dr. Chazov, personal physician to Leonid Brezhnev! There are many, many more examples one could give. And all these professional groups are increasingly vocal, coordinated, well financed, and effective.

But what could a visitor from outer space make of such a puzzling contradiction? Not being human and not having experienced life on Earth under human control, they could find no rational answer.

But we can. We can because we have created the present conditions of polarisation and extremity, and because the solutions to the problems arising from separateness and selfishness—which create wrong relationships—depend upon the essential nature of mankind itself and upon our willingness to correct and redeem what we have spoiled, contaminated and debased. Not easy; particularly in the light of so many self-righteous and intransigent attitudes—but it can be done.

It seems to me that there is a first and primary objective upon which all else may well depend, and that a keynote theme we have used frequently over recent years pinpoints a basic factor in world need and is of particular relevance today. The keynote is: The fate of men and nations is determined by the values which govern their decisions.

Essentially all attitudes and actions tie back to accepted values and standards of behaviour. And one does not expect that the peoples of all the many and varied cultures, nations, races, religions and social strata will accept identical values and adhere to similar behavioural patterns. But there are good and better, and bad and worse, in every culture, in every circumstance, and in personal standards, for everyone to choose. And we have the right and the responsibility of choice, and it seems that for too long we have accepted and lived by standards that degrade the quality of life, that undermine moral and ethical values, and that increasingly bring us into conflict with others—other people, other groupings, other nations; and with the whole ecological system of the planet. Our standards have remained materialistic and self-centred beyond the time when the values of materialism—and there are values—and the lessons of self-centredness should have been learned and left behind.

When differences of opinion and of values clash and confront one another, confrontation too often leads to conflict rather than to conference and conciliation. And we seem to be bogged down in a cycle of conflict now—or perhaps it is more a vicious circle than a cycle—because no nation seems to have the courage, the political daring, to break out of it by new revolutionary thinking, and by action which may go against the popular and familiar current. But if not reversed, the present trends all point to the ultimate disaster of nuclear catastrophe.

So how do we, the people—insignificant and without any obvious influence—get to grips on a large enough scale with these world issues? Or even at the level of local communities? Where are the answers to be found?

In detailed working out, the answers are complex and manifold. But even so, they reduce down to one basic fundamental fact: to the essential nature of mankind itself. And this is an ages-old puzzle with no one permanent or complete answer and which no political, economic or military power cares to address. Neither do the religions of the world—which prefer to perpetuate the unknowable nature of the mysteries with which they have surrounded the relationship between God and man—offer any satisfactory pointers.

Psychology attempts in different ways to answer the question: "What is man that Thou (God) art mindful of him?" But most systems of psychology skate on the surface, analyse and dig into the subconscious, or examine the effects rather than the causes of basic problems, and thereby fail to penetrate to the reality. The same is true of philosophy which tends to equate man with the contents of his reasoning mind. Perhaps science comes closer today to understanding the true constitution of man by the realisation that all is energy," and that a human being is a coherent, integrated, interdependent unit of energy—electricity—intricately, delicately, but perfectly balanced, so that, in mint condition, each part moves in cooperation and harmony with all other parts.

But even that explains only the physical mechanism, which is truly the tip of the iceberg, that part of the microcosmic world which can be seen and known, while the rest remains as mysterious as the unseen and the intangible always appear to be.

One of the.great developments of this technological century, however, is that along with the researches and developments of concrete science, physical science, a new science has been born, quietly and without fanfare—*the science of the initiates*. This is the science of those who know, through personal experience, that each and every human being is a spark of divinity clothed in form, a fragment of the one Life (God), embedded in mental, emotional and physical substance. This permeation of matter by the living energy of the Godhead is partly for the purpose of experience, but essentially in order to redeem the substance, or the materiality, of our planet through the use of a totally different scale of values or state of consciousness, applied to the problems of human relationships and world reconstruction.

This new science is known by many names. Its true name is: *the science of the initiates*, because it is through a series of expansions in consciousness, producing liberation into a fuller state of awareness, and into an enlarged field of knowledge and of light, that God immanent in every form of life achieves an ascendency over that form, so liberating its atomic matter. These expansions in consciousness, and entry into greater light, are called *initiations* because they provide entry into hitherto unknown states of conscious awareness; but they are initiations due to the choice, the effort, and the growth in understanding of each one. They are not "conferred" by agencies outside the personal self as a reward or a recognition, or as a condition of entry into some hitherto sealed or secret order.

Other names for this science include the "science of esotericism" and the "science of redemption." It is a science because the way to achieve its goals is well known to many who, over the centuries, have "charted" that way by providing guidelines and techniques which we can learn, test and apply for ourselves, techniques that work. The Laws and Principles which underlie the evolutionary processes on this planet are eternal and verifiable, although the ways these Laws and Principles should be worked out in daily life vary and change with the changing condition of human consciousness and the variations in human and world problems and relationships. These Laws and Principles for the Age of Aquarius are said to be:

1. The Law of Right Human Relations.

2. The Principle of Goodwill.

3. The Law of Group Endeavour.

4. The Principle of Unanimity.

5. The Law of Spiritual Approach.

6. The Principle of Essential Divinity.

Essentially there is one overriding goal and this applies to every aspect of esoteric science. This goal can be stated in a few words, although it may take centuries to accomplish. That goal is for each one, through individual personal experience and growth, "to tread this way the ways of men and know the ways of God." In other words, to bring God transcendent in His universe, and God immanent in man, into a fully conscious, alive, cooperative and creative relationship. By so doing one can begin to contribute to planetary evolution. One becomes a co-creator with God, with our planetary Logos.

And if this is so, and if the redemptive, esoteric science of the initiates is really factual, then there are several logical conclusions to be drawn, two or which are:

(1) that, since there is one life force—the God in us—which ensouls and energises all forms in all kingdoms, including the human, the fact that we are one humanity occupying one world has a much deeper and more powerful basis than the mere fact of our physical—economic and material—interdependence. And

(2) that there must be kingdoms in nature lying above or beyond the state of consciousness of the human kingdom just as there are also subhuman kingdoms—the animal, the vegetable, or the plant, and the mineral. It is from the "superhuman" kingdoms that the techniques of the science of the initiates are made available to humanity.

The major focal point for the transmission of knowledge, love and wisdom, to humanity, is the fifth kingdom—that centre of consciousness lying immediately ahead of our own present stage of unfoldment and awareness. The fifth kingdom is better known, perhaps, as the kingdom of souls or, in Christian terminology, the kingdom of heaven. It is into this state of total soul awareness, unrestricted by the limitations of an imperfect personality, that the science of the initiates eventually admits us, progressively, and over a long period of time. The members of this fifth kingdom are all liberated human beings who have freed themselves from personality control, who have purified and redeemed thereby the portions of "unredeemed" planetary substance in their own beings for which they were responsible, and who therefore function in full consciousness as exponents of the God immanent within them. In other words, in them the balance has been struck and the relationships created between God and man. This is really the biblical story of the prodigal son who left his "father's house" for the far country, learned the emptiness and discontent of a life devoid of spiritual values, and eventually decided to "arise and go" back to the source of his being. This is the spiritual journey of all of us.

The point is that this is a *conscious* journey, a conscious choice, which we all make at a certain stage of development. The way back is long, involving life after life; it is hard, demanding constant vigilance, self-discipline and self-sacrifice. But when a sufficient element of the soul's light and love are alive in us, the urge to good and the will to love and to serve humanity become so strong that the difficulties of the personal self fall below the level of consciousness, and from that time on the pace is quickened, the life of service becomes more usefully effective, and more joyous— and the process of initiation is then well underway.

The fifth kingdom in nature is known also as the spiritual Hierarchy of the planet; a hierarchy because there are different stages of evolutionary unfoldment represented in that kingdom as there are within humanity itself. In fact, the stages of consciousness within the Hierarchy range from that of the soul-infused disciple newly accepted within the periphery of the Hierarchy, to the unique state of consciousness of the Christ himself, centred as the "heart of love," the focal point of energy reception, within the Hierarchy.

This fifth kingdom is also the planetary heart centre, because the dominant quality of energy focussed there is the energy of pure love, the quality and nature of the life force itself. And the fully redeemed human beings who serve within it are known as the Masters of the Wisdom and the Lords of Compassion, because they have become both wise and compassionate as they free themselves from human separateness and selfishness. They are concerned with the right evolutionary development and the right relationships of the human and the subhuman kingdoms, and with global issues of world reconstruction and right relationship between the peoples and the nations of the world. They are practical, intensely active, and totally committed centres of light and energy, contemporary and forward-looking; they are not the nonsensical, vague, wishy-washy, or authoritarian characters so often held out to us by some groups who claim to be in constant contact with them all, and to be responsible for interpreting their wishes and directives through endless communications. They look for creative intelligence and love in practical working disciples. They are not interested in believers or followers or, as it has been expressed, in "stupid sheep or silly saints." They need cooperators and workers of initiative and responsibility. Their outer contact with humanity is limited at present. They work behind the scenes, impressing the minds of disciples with a vision of the future and of the Plan for humanity in a broad and general sense, the Plan of light and love which disciples themselves are then left entirely free to express correctly according to current circumstances and needs.

It is expected, however, that certain members of the spiritual Hierarchy are preparing to move outward again into physical form in order to help speed the transition process into the new age. But they will still work without claims, without claim making, and without recognition from the majority of human beings. As this externalisation takes place, so also new teaching and training esoteric schools will come into existence, schools of initiation, schools concerned with the processes of an expanding consciousness which lead into the various initiations possible to humanity. Much of the present esoteric teaching on the soul and on the constitution of man, for example, and the process of evolution, will by then have become absorbed into the normal academic curricula, and new esoteric teachings will be given in two grades of schools, preparatory and advanced. It seems that these two grades of schools of initiation, of which there will be six, function in relation with one another. Although they are called preparatory and advanced, neither one is either superior or inferior to the other, they function in complete interrelationship. You will perhaps be interested to know that one of the preparatory schools will be founded in Sweden with its more advanced counterpart in Russia. All this is according to the unfolding Plan for humanity.

The Plan for humanity is the immediate concern of the spiritual Hierarchy of the planet. The Plan, so far as the Hierarchy is concerned, is an energy formula—a plan of love and light, expressing the power of a will-to-good for the world as a whole. *How* these energies of love and light are interpreted and applied to current situations is our human responsibility; we are free to work as we choose. The Plan today means, essentially, that through our ability to introduce the spiritual values of cooperation and sharing into a divided world and a selfish materialism, the love and the unity which do underlie the happenings of the time may break through into a position of greater influence in determining the way ahead.

We are already intelligent in a strictly material way; we are *becoming* creatively intelligent in a more spiritual sense as the light of the Plan, the light of the soul, penetrates our consciousness. The love needed to transform intelligence into wisdom is fully released by response to the soul and to the Hierarchy, by a response of love and service for all humanity, a love for all forms of life in which the same spark of divinity, the same life force, is present. Love is the synthesising factor and right human relationships are love on a world scale.

That love is actively present in such countries as your own, Sweden, and in Switzerland, for example, where, through neutrality and inclusiveness, service can be rendered to other nations in times of crisis, and this is significant and indicative of spiritual responsibilities. Sweden has given generously to the world of her loving soul through the brilliant service of many of her sons and daughters. I'm thinking of two or three in particular. For instance, the outstanding example of Dag Hammarskjold whom I have heard several times address the General Assembly of the United Nations. I'm thinking of those two remarkable people, Gunnar and Alva Myrdal. I'm also thinking of Inga Thorssen, whom I heard speak recently at the United Nations when she gave the keynote address at a conference and who, at the same time, received a peace award from the World Spiritual University. These people represent and speak for the soul of their nation. Nations, like individuals, respond to the soul principle, depending on their state of spiritual unfoldment. All nations have a responsibility, a contribution, a service, and a destiny to work out in relation to the world community of nations. That there may often be an element of self-interest and expedience present in service is no doubt true, for we are still imperfect. But an example is there, an example from which we can all draw inspiration as we seek to translate spiritual values and the inner spiritual unity, which is, into a way of establishing right international relationships.

This *reality* of human unity and relationship with all forms of life in all kingdoms is perhaps the most significant issue we face today. How can that subjective reality become an objective achievement? How can we solve our many divisive problems of race, territory, militarism, terrorism, aggression, economics, religions, culture, political selfishness—which all bind back to a basic sense of separativeness—until we give factual, practical recognition to a fundamental spiritual unity? This underlying reality of spiritual oneness assures that all separative actions eventually boomerang; that all expressions of hatred and narrow self-interest, damaging to others, lock the perpetrator into a prison of his own making and eventually rebound to his own loss. For in the unified spiritual structure which is characteristic of our planet, we all gain and progress together or we all lose. And this is one of the as yet unlearned lessons with which we have been faced from the time humanity as a race, as a planetary centre of energy, appeared on this planet. We don't yet evaluate loss and gain in terms of values and principles but only in terms of things and desires—power, prestige and possessions. And I want to quote this to you from one of Alice Bailey's books: "On a world scale the world disciple, humanity, is today on the verge of a major awakening and joint registration of a unity not hitherto reached; the growth of the spirit of internationalism, the inclusiveness of the scientific attitude, and the spread of a universal humanitarian welfare movement are all indicative of this meeting place."

We have been asked to "work aggressively for unity" in order to offset the aggressive effects of separateness and selfishness. To "work aggressively" means to work with drive and determination, with vision and initiative, without discouragement or frustration; in other words, with our normal personality reactions completely under control and subordinated to the soul task of creating unity and establishing right human relationships in our own environment, whatever that may be. And this is really all that is asked of us. We are all of various stations in life, occupied in different professions, trades or vocations. We have varied opportunities to express what we know and what we believe, and to act on the values we accept and practice. And this extensive variety, permeating the whole range of human consciousness, is of real value to the working out of the Plan. It is the acceptance of personal responsibility, under whatever circumstances, in whatever place, for the introduction of new values and the revelation of human unity which guarantees the success of the divine Plan.

Better values to live by, and conscious choices where those values are concerned, start always on an individual scale. As *people,* living beings, intimately involved in all humankind, we affect the whole structure by the way we think and the way we act. In the last analysis, concern is not enough, commitment is required. An attitude of "it all depends on me" is a healthy one so long as no self-importance accompanies it. There are hundreds of thousands, no millions, of disciples, aspirants, and men and women of goodwill around the world working today to the limit of their capacity and it is these workers who can, with that little extra effort one can always make, transform human attitudes, influence human decisions and set the world on a new course of right human relationships leading to peace on Earth.

Does it sound too little? Perhaps, but that famous journey of a thousand miles began with its first step many, many years ago and progress has been made over the centuries in spite of the outer appearance of an increased condition of crisis and conflict. These crises are intensified as spiritual energies come into conflict with retrogressive materialism and crisis points are times of unequalled opportunity. The soul of humanity is in stronger control of its personality instrument than even a century or two ago and this is a continuing spiritual experience—a emergence. Growth, once achieved, is maintained, and continued— never lost. We can add to what has been achieved by our own efforts. We can act and we can serve; we should not preach and we cannot teach, except by example. We can literally revolutionise our environment by our attitude of mind and heart, by the values we accept and live by, and by our personal commitment to the working out of the Plan for humanity equally administered for the whole human race. And this is all summed up in these words of this well known affirmation, the Mantram of Unification:

The sons of men are one and I am one with them.
I seek to love, not hate;
I seek to serve and not exact due service;
I seek to heal, not hurt.

Let pain bring due reward of light and love.
Let the soul control the outer form,
And life, and all events,
And bring to light the Love
That underlies the happenings of the time.

Let vision come and insight.
Let the future stand revealed.
Let inner union demonstrate and outer cleavages be gone.
Let love prevail.
Let all men love.

CHAPTER 3 — Christ As He Is — A Supreme Spiritual Executive*

We are holding this seminar today because the reappearance of the Christ is "imminent," and much glamour, confusion and false claims are attached to the idea. If, in discussion and meditation today, we can cut through the glamour and the illusion surrounding the Christ and the Hierarchy and reveal the reality of the Christ "as he is" in his planetary service, we will let light into the whole situation and create a thoughtform more in keeping with the truth.

The reappearance of the Christ is "imminent" only in the time sense of the Hierarchy, which could mean decades or centuries to us, who have no real concept of the eternity registered by the celestial timeclock. In fact, however, the event is measurable in our terms as "the foreseeable future." But some of us can see no further than tomorrow or next year; while others occupy their minds and their creative attention with the new world of the twenty-first century; and still others with the 2,500 years of the Aquarian age. So the actual timing of the Christ's reappearance is still unknown to humanity, except that we do know the conditions that must prevail in the world before the Christ, under law, can reappear.

It has been said in Alice Bailey's book, *The Reappearance of the Christ*, that if we look for the Christ as he was two thousand years ago, we will fail to recognise him when he reappears to continue his work in the Aquarian age. This gives us an invaluable clue; because, like ourselves and all other forms of life, the

---

* Keynote address at the Seminar on "The Reappearance of the Christ" in New York, December 12, 1981.

147

Christ is subject to the Laws of Evolution and, therefore, to inevitable change and development. It may
seem to us that the already perfect cannot be improved.
But perfection is relative; and even our planetary
Logos, our God, is evolving at His own cosmic level
and in relation to His responsibilities within the solar
system and the universe.

Humanity has evolved in consciousness during the
past two thousand years in obvious and extraordinary ways; the Christ, too, has evolved, and both he
and his work during the period of his next incarnation—
whether long or short—will reflect that change in consciousness. When he resumes his direct contact with
human affairs, he will no longer be confined to one
small area of the planet, or to the teaching function
which seemed to be his main avenue of service in
Palestine. His vision, his influence and his activities
will be planetary, and will affect human thought and
activity in all the main areas of human life; although
he may well concentrate his major attention and energy
in one or other of the specific avenues of daily living.

It is in this sense that we shall recognise the evolved
state of the Christ consciousness in the modern world—
by the potency of his world influence and the skill in
action of his directed energies. We are asked "to see
the Christ as he is" and, in the work of preparation
for his reappearance, to reveal him in his true role as
the world server in Aquarius, wielding an influence
through his disciples in all parts of the world and in
all areas of life. For in this new planetary role, and at
his dramatic turning point in history, he needs the
cooperation of every enlightened mind and every loving heart everywhere.

There are today many who accept the basic idea of
the Christ's reappearance as a potent influence in
human consciousness, thereby affecting human behaviour and world affairs, but who place upon him a limi-
tation of their own minds by refusing to accept the

possibility of an actual physical being—a human being, as we are. But we know that the Christ is both human and divine, the first member of the human race to reconcile that duality in himself, and to become God/man in manifestation. Hence his unique role in planetary affairs. And we are definitely given to understand that the Christ's reappearance will include not only the mental and emotional planes by the stimulation of human minds and hearts, but also the physical plane. According to the Bailey books, it was humanity's own decision to fight out the world war (1914-1945) upon the physical plane, rather than on the mental level of ideas and ideologies, where it could have been contained, which determined the Christ's decision to include the physical plane in his sphere of Aquarian operations. We so often forget, don't we, how absolutely interconnected and interdependent all life is, and the extent to which our own thoughts and feelings and actions determine the outcome of larger planetary issues of which we may not even be aware.

The threefold method of the Christ's reappearance is put to us in these words adapted from the book, *The Rays and the Initiations*, pp. 615-620:

First. He will reappear by an "overshadowing" and telepathic influence on the minds of prepared disciples and initiates. This will be his primary work on the mental plane and the most effective method for his "spiritual interference" in world affairs. Thus he will have outposts of his consciousness in every nation.

Second. By stimulating the Christ life, or consciousness, within the masses of humanity, leading to a reorientation of human desire; this involves the astral, or emotional, plane. As goodwill is released into the hearts of mankind, they become more disposed to create right human relationships—which is the major objective of the Christ's triple activity.

And third. By his physical appearance, so establishing a potent point of hierarchical energy on Earth in a way not previously possible. The locale of this focal point is not yet determined; it depends upon the effects of the first two stages; it depends also upon the medium he will use to implement his new purpose — whether politics, religion, economics, the social sciences. The determining factor will be "the number, the ability, and the status of the disciples active in the chosen field."

So let us at least assume the possibility of a physical person, a Christ, working on the world stage to introduce the values, the guidelines and the *modus operandi* of the age of Aquarius.

This will mean a totally new development in human and planetary experience. There have been avatars in incarnation for brief periods at several times over the centuries. Hermes, Krishna, Buddha, and the Christ of two thousand years ago, are a few of those who have brought light and change into the world by manifesting an aspect of divinity during a world period of lawlessness and degeneration. But the Christ has now achieved a state of spiritual unfoldment which, for the first time, permits a Son of God to manifest all three aspects of the God-head simultaneously — light, the light of the creative intelligence unfolded in the past; love, the major influence and energy wielded by our planetary Logos for the unfoldment of manifested life in the present; and power, the power of the will-to-good, motivating all logoic activity and infusing all human souls with the quality to be revealed in the future.

So today, in his planetary role as representative of "the Father," the Christ unites the past, the present and the future; the whole and the part; the One and the many; the subjective, spiritual life and its objective, concretised expression. The Christ embodies, therefore, the essence and the meaning of right relationship, and this is his keynote for the coming era, just as the theme of RELATIONSHIP is, inevitably, the controlling motive of our planetary Life, with Whom the Christ is identified and Whom he represents.

This presupposes a unique function within the whole planetary structure. The "office" of the Christ is a set and stable centre, the "heart of Love" within the Hierarchy, the planetary heart. Yet his function is as both "head" and "heart" of this centre, the great Ashram of Sanat Kumara. He establishes the alignment and the point of tension within the Hierarchy which provides the three aspects of the God-head, focussed in Shamballa, with receptive, responsive points of energy transmission. His esoteric relationship with all forms of life, and his identification with the living energy which animates those forms, has activated a permanent centre in Hierarchy and closed a gap in the planetary alignment, which only a spiritual executive of the stature of the Christ — God/man — could accomplish. This is his "office" in a spiritual and subjective sense.

It is an office (given the name of "Christ") just as the Chairman or President of a company is an office, held by different individuals at different times. The function of the focal point at the centre of each of the forty-nine ashrams within the Hierarchy — the Master — is also similar to the function of the various heads of departments in an organisation. All are points of energy reception and distribution within areas of accepted responsibility in relation to the work to be done.

What of the external work of the Christ among humanity; how does, or will, his divine manhood manifest; and how can we prepare to see the Christ "as he is"?

One of the outstanding characteristics of all spiritual development is its inclusiveness. Nothing of any value is left behind or discarded; everything of significance to the process of evolution is built into the consciousness, or the memory bank, while only the harmful, the unworthy and the unnecessary are discarded and left behind, having served their temporary purposes in the duality of human experience. This means that as an individual becomes more "spiritual," more attuned to the divine principle ensouling him, he also becomes more human, a more accurate example of what a redeemed and enlightened human being is meant to be.

In the Christ, spirit and matter converge and achieve their common identity. Therefore, as a perfected "Son of God," the Christ has also perfected his humanity and will be able to demonstrate before the eyes and ears of the world as he reappears what it means to be truly human. And this, I suggest, is the basic difference between the life and work of the Christ two thousand years ago and his life and work in the coming age. In Palestine, for the Piscean era, he needed to demonstrate his divinity and power; today there is no need for miracles and for the manifestation of powers mystifying to humanity. For Aquarian men and women he will demonstrate his perfected humanity in expressing the will and the purpose of deity, symbolising the ability of present-day mankind "to restore the Plan on Earth." His coming will concern and affect all humanity and his field of service will include world affairs and global problems. It is said that the main focus of Christ's attention has yet to be determined — by him; it will depend, not on what we, humanity, might consider to be the area of greatest human misery and need, but on the extent of the preparatory work undertaken in some vital aspect of human life, and on the numbers of prepared disciples available in that field.

Contrary to popular belief, the Christ is not coming to correct our mistakes and take care of the appalling results of our own separateness and willful selfishness. He is not returning as a great religious leader; the religions of the world are too divided and factionalised to accept the Christ's inclusiveness and love for all mankind. He is coming to establish the principles and values, including the techniques, on which life must be based during the Aquarian age, and to encourage the present incipient trend towards right relationships—leading to peace on Earth—due to unfold in the coming two thousand year cycle.

Wherever these objectives can best be nurtured, the Christ will work. Obviously, therefore, he could emerge as a vital force in any field: in education; in government—legislative, judicial, or executive; in science; in business; in economics; in social affairs; in religion. He could be black, brown, olive, yellow or white; man or woman. We do not yet know. We know only that adequate preparation must be made for his coming work in all fields; a balance created, both in world relationships and affairs, in economic and political matters, and within the minds of human beings; some degree of world peace must be established as the demonstration of a "gained wisdom" in human relationships; and there must be sufficient numbers of trained, serving and dedicated disciples available to act as his cooperators and co-workers. Here is a true definition of the new group of world servers, who factually function today as the forerunners of the Christ.

He will not be publicly proclaimed as the Christ, either before or after his emergence on the world scene; and he, himself, will not claim that distinction. He will work as an enlightened and capable individual of vision and purpose, and he will be recognised by his "own people."

The Christ will be preceded by certain members of the spiritual Hierarchy, members of some of the forty-nine ashrams, who will also help to complete the final preparations for his future work. This phase in the externalisation process, we are told, should be completed by about the year 2025; after that, we should be alert to recognise the Christ—wherever he may choose to reappear—by his work, by the world influence he wields, and by the radiatory and magnetic effects of this truly unique and extraordinary God/man, which will be seen and heard worldwide over radio and television, evoking recognition and response from perceptive minds and hearts.

This is the Christ "as he is," not as he was two thousand years ago. He is a world server, a world spiritual executive, involved in the complex affairs of our contemporary society in process of great change, undergoing the crises and tensions of a transformation in consciousness, which the Christ has also experienced in himself. He returns as a representative of the great Life ensouling this planet, bringing with him the Power, the Love and the Light of the Godhead, expertly adjusted to human capacity to receive and use, and to the detailed complexities of life on Earth as a human being.

The Christ is indeed a supreme spiritual executive. We would do well so to focus our innermost attention towards him and his mission that our minds and hearts will come to know him as he is, so providing him with the direct links into the contemporary scene which will guarantee the successful outcome of his planetary service in the years ahead. World reconstruction and world transformation depend upon the cooperative work of responsible men and women working with the Christ. We, too, can take our place in that group of "Christ's own people." Let recognition be the aim!

Finally, let the words of the Master Djwhal Khul strengthen our understanding of the inevitable working out of the law:

"It is to the whole world that Christ comes and not just to the Christian world. He comes to the East and to the West, and has foreseen this 'time of the end' with its planetary catastrophes, phenomenal disasters, despair and invocation—arising from both the East and the West. He knew that in the time of final crisis and tension, humanity itself would force His emergence." (*The Reappearance of the Christ*, p. 100).

"We have now reached a point where the inevitability of Christ's return is established, scientifically and under law; this constitutes a call which He may not deny and which He must obey. . . . [When] the hearts of men, the heart of the planet, i.e., the Hierarchy, and the heart of the Hierarchy, the Christ, are in a state of positive contact; when this channel is open and unobstructed, then the Christ *will* come. Nothing can stop his appearance. . . . This alignment, when effectively concluded, will bring about a clear channel or pathway of return or line of light or magnetic power, between:

1. The centre where the Will of God is known, Shamballa.

2. The Hierarchy, the planetary heart centre.

3. The Christ, the heart of love within the Hierarchy.

4. The initiates, disciples and aspirants who form the new group of world servers, seeking to embody the love and light needed in the world today.

5. The hearts of men and women of goodwill in all lands who are responsive to love expressed through right human relations.

6. The focal point through which the Lord of Love will work on Earth. . . . Thus from the highest manifestation of Deity, down to its appearance through the medium of some focal point in our modern world, a 'structure of approach' and a 'path of return' are being constructed which will bring the long awaited Christ into our midst. Nothing can stop or prevent his return." (Adapted from *The Rays and the Initiations*, pp. 618-20.)

How clearly that sixfold progression of divine love tells us what still remains to be accomplished through the power and the energy of love; we need more love between peoples, love between nations—a heart "open on the world"—love uniting the great planetary centres, Shamballa/Hierarchy/Humanity. For, with the direct impact of the Shamballa force into humanity during this century, the second aspect of the first ray of Will or Power (the Shamballa force) can be expressed on Earth for the first time. The Christ, with the assistance of the Hierarchy, is the "distributing Aspect and directing Factor" for this potency—the power of the Will-to-Good—and it is this Power that will begin to manifest when he appears. This is the true reason for the Christ's intention to reappear; to manifest the power and the synthesis of the one Life. This will reveal a clear distinction between material living and spiritual living; it will become apparent through a widespread demonstration of human goodwill, the lowest expression of the second ray of Love/Wisdom, strengthened by the Will-to-Good of the first ray.

Much depends, therefore, on an understanding use of the power of love, as the Christ combines his esoteric planetary work with his exoteric world service. We can cooperate in both aspects of the Christ's executive function in the coming years with understanding and commitment.

"We know, O Lord of Life and Love, about the need. Touch our hearts anew with love that we, too, may love and give."

CHAPTER 4—Preparation for the Reappearance of the Christ*

With all the teaching and information on the reappearance of the Christ given in the Master D.K.'s books, and all the articles and comments appearing increasingly over recent years, one might wonder what more can be said about something of which, in reality, we know so little.

I want to base this conference address on the Reflective Meditation on Preparation for the Reappearance of the Christ. This is a meditation in worldwide use by growing numbers of people; it is creating a momentum within the work of preparation—the preparation of men's minds and hearts. It is in human *consciousness* that the Christ will first reveal his eternal presence; therefore, it is in human consciousness that the necessary conditions for his return must be established. This must obviously involve subjective work—meditation within the soul-infused minds of a subjectively unified group of world servers.

This special meditation was first given to us in the early 1940's. It is included in the second volume of the book *Discipleship in the New Age* (pp. 226-8), and forms the first part of a two-fold piece of meditative work. Both relate to the present period of preparation for the Christ's reappearance. Both are "redemptive" in effect—as they infuse the substance of the three worlds of human evolution with dynamic energy. One of the major hindrances to the work of preparation is the shortage of money for the work; the second meditation is therefore focussed on "Attracting

---

* Address given at the Arcane School Conference in Geneva, Switzerland, June 1979.

Money for Hierarchical Purposes." And this meditation, used with the meditation on Preparation for the
Reappearance of the Christ, can and does help to
rechannel money energy into the hands of those who
have accepted responsibility for the sustained, difficult task of preparation during a world period as materialistic and as selfishly oriented as the present.

It is suggested that the "Reappearance" meditation should be used on Thursday, every week—Thursday is a second ray day, the spiritual high point of
the week; and the "Money" meditation on Sundays—
Sunday is a first ray day. This combination of first
and second rays is important in esoteric work. It
establishes an invocative/evocative effect in consciousness and what has been called an essential condition for successful work—the relationship between
need, love and magnetic power. Too often the would-
be esoteric server finds difficulty in handling one ray
type of energy when his line of least resistance lies
more with another. But these two, the first and second rays, are really the primary types of energy for
us and we can all learn to work with them. We function normally in relation to the third ray of intelligent activity, which governs the planet Earth during
this world cycle; but the task is to function with equal
facility in relationship with those two streams of
energy which will one day absorb and incorporate all
other "lesser energies," the second ray of Love/Wisdom
and the first ray of Purposeful Will.

Another outstanding value in these two special
redemptive meditations lies in their dependence on
the Great Invocation. The stages in the "Reappearance" meditation are based on the first three stanzas
of the Invocation, while the fourth stanza is incorporated into the "Money" meditation. This is sufficient
reason in itself for the regular use of both, because
"the most important part" of the work of preparation
for the reappearance of the Christ is "teaching men

on a large scale" to use the Invocation. This, of course, means our own personal use also; and it has been, for many years, incorporated into every aspect of our group work so that what the Invocation embodies and signifies occupies a central position in all we do. Preparation for the reappearance of the Christ, in general, and in particular through the use of the Great Invocation, forms the framework and provides the motivation and incentive for our *raison d'être*. That aspect of hierarchical work for which we have accepted responsibility, at the request of the Master Djwhal Khul, is involved in the preparatory work of the great ashram of Sanat Kumara. The responsibility is awesome seen in this light; but it is also sweetened and empowered by the love flowing through the planetary heart.

There is one further point of interest about these redemptive meditations before we move on into their presented form. Each one is described as a "Reflective" meditation. A different technique is used to the accustomed Patanjali method of Raja Yoga — meditation with a "seed" thought. In these special meditations the mind is lifted into a contemplative attitude, a condition in which it can most easily "reflect" reality, that which exists, or IS, on the plane of the higher, abstract mind, as well as reflecting what is present on the level of the creative intelligence of the observing, concrete mind. We can "reflect on" conditions in the three worlds of human consciousness and at the same time act as a "reflector" of the conditions to be created according to the Plan-inspired energies centred within the spiritual Hierarchy. In this way one can bring together, or relate, what *is* at a lower level of consciousness with *what should be* according to the spiritual possibilities inherent in the soul of humanity. This is transmutation, or redemption; the substitution of the greater for the lesser, the higher for the lower, of the spiritual for the material. And this redemptive process in substance, carried forward over a long period of time by a growing group of experienced and dedicated esoteric servers, is infallible. Human hearts and minds are inspired, are changed, are prepared for the coming of the Christ. The work is done.

As we set to work with the Reflective Meditation on Preparation for the Reappearance of the Christ, we first ask ourselves, as personalities, three questions. These questions are intended to focus attention and align the personality on the mental plane, but they should be answered *in the light of the soul*. The questions are: "As a member of the new group of world servers, what is my specific, focussed intention at this moment of dedicated contact with my soul? Is my concentrated and expressed personality purpose in line with hierarchical intention—as far as I am permitted to know it? Have I—in my own personal daily life—earned the right (because of definite effort and not so much because of success) to stand with those servers who are now undertaking the work of preparation?

These are serious, searching questions if we give them the attention which is their due. They go to the heart of our personal and personality attitudes and actions. But having answered them, we can then assume the dedicated attitude of the pledged disciple, with this affirmation:

"Forgetting the things which lie behind, I will strive towards my higher spiritual possibilities. I dedicate myself anew to the service of the Coming One and will do all I can to prepare men's minds and hearts for that event. I have no other life intention."

I have occasionally heard a doubt voiced over that final commitment. As personalities there may be a variety of things which we intend to do with our lives, many of them worthy and valuable. But *as a soul*, knowing that the soul, the real disciple, is concerned only with the Plan of Hierarchy, what other life intention could there be except to cooperate with what is present in the consciousness of the planetary heart centre as it carries the life, the energy, and the Purpose of the planetary Logos through the Plan into the consciousness of the centre humanity? And today the planetary Life is focussed on that great and imminent event—the reappearance of the Christ. It is a rising tide of planetary attention of which we are all a part.

The meditation itself falls into four main stages, following a brief pause after the affirmation of life intention. In this pause the consciousness is lifted and focussed at the highest, contemplative level of the mental plane. From that high point we are asked first "to visualise the world situation as best you can .... See the mass of men everywhere glowing with a dim light, and here and there, points of brighter light where members of the new group of world servers and men of spiritual intention and of loving hearts are working for their fellowmen." We then visualise "the vivid light of the Hierarchy streaming towards humanity and slowly merging with the light which is already in men." As we do so we sound the first stanza of the Great Invocation.

From this it is clear that we are asked and expected to work as the Hierarchy works; to see world conditions and human affairs in terms of light or lack of light; to realise that the new world order, which is the main preoccupation of the Christ as he reappears, depends upon the irradiation of the substance of the mental plane with spiritual energy, vision and inspiration, on "enlightened" attitudes of mind as a guarantee for right action.

We might recall the Tibetan's reference over thirty years ago (*The Rays and the Initiations*, p. 430) to the "heavy overshadowing cloud" involving the Near and Middle East, parts of Eastern Europe, Egypt, the Arab States, Palestine and Russia. Today, in 1979, this is still a dark area on the face of the Earth, with representative human problems concentrated in the religious, political and territorial relationships and institutions of the countries concerned. The Tibetan asks, "Can that cloud be dissipated by . . . right thinking and planning . . . or must it break in disaster over the world?"

This "cloud", in common with all other darkened areas of human consciousness, can be dissipated by "right thinking", that is, by meditation and the ability to channel and direct light energy. Such a channeling is needed today to help clear the mental atmosphere of human thought, where action originates. And in this special meditation we have the perfect tool for our use.

We realise, too, that the spiritual Hierarchy, as a lighted and fully awakened centre within the planetary body, is directing its energies towards humanity which is today more characterised by the "dark light" of matter than by the radiance of the anchored Christ principle, the soul. Yet that potential exists in all mankind, offering to the inflowing lighted energy a redemptive opportunity. Light, streaming forth into the minds of men, will transform consciousness, change the patterns of human behaviour, establish an era of better relationships between the peoples of the world, and permit the Christ to function effectively in the mental atmosphere of the human family.

In our meditation we are next asked to "ponder upon the reappearance of the Christ. Realise that no matter by what name he may be called in the many world religions, he is still the same great Identity. Reflect and speculate upon the possible results of his appearance." And at this point we sound the second stanza of the Invocation.

Here true contemplation comes into action, involving the intuition, the buddhic faculty of pure love, fused with the higher mind. What will be the Christ's outstanding quality and therefore his major effect within the world of men? As "the embodiment of the

Principle of Love", he represents the nature of our planetary Life during this world cycle, a love nature so wise and enlightened, so truly aligned with the will-to-good of logoic Purpose, that the Christ principle in the human heart will be stimulated, by his Presence, from latency into potency. The all-inclusive consciousness of the Christ will find outlets and reflected impacts throughout all areas of human life. Loving understanding will come to be known as a positive force in the building of a new world, as the cornerstone of right human relationships and as an enduring strength in the persistent day-to-day efforts to restore peace and security, a sound economy, freedom from hunger and want, to all peoples everywhere. Love, streaming forth into the hearts of men, unites mankind with the planetary heart, the Hierarchy, and with the Christ himself. His work in the new age will be increasingly effective in practical terms as this redemptive process accelerates and the hearts of men and women everywhere open to one another with a concern equal to that given to self-interest and personal progress.

This should be the outstanding effect of the Christ's work in Aquarius—the tendency to unite the peoples of the world in cooperative, practical endeavour directed towards the right solution of human and world problems.

The next phase of the meditation is of equal importance: "Endeavour to concentrate your fixed intention to serve and to spread love in your surroundings and realise that *insofar as you can do these things* you are attempting to blend your personal will with the divine Will."

These words make it quite clear that the will of God, so far as humanity is concerned, is that we should love and serve, and that these qualities must be *expressed* in our "surroundings." It is so easy to love in the abstract, but meaningless in a world so crystallised in form that only "concretised" energy can create the necessary effects. To love and serve in the place where we are, charges the words with meaning and significance, gives them life and reality and, at the same time, impresses on us the difficult and magical requirements of real discipleship—one who is "expert in the life of the soul", one whose horizontal life of service fully expresses his vertical realisations.

This requirement calls in the spiritual will, the highest aspect of the soul. The first step towards the achievement of pure love and true service, as the soul knows these attributes, is the *will*-to-love and the *will*-to-serve. When the spiritual will is present, active and in control, then the "little will" of the personality directed to its own ends, fades out and the greater good floods in.

The wording of this phase of the meditation is therefore deceptively simple. To love and to serve in our own environment as a disciple and in the practical terms which all those who serve the Christ and work for his reappearance must express, demands of us all the light, the love and the selfless will of which our souls are capable. Using the third stanza of the Great Invocation, we therefore invoke energy from the centre where the Will of God is known that Purpose, God's Purpose for His whole creation, may redirect and transmute the self-will of man, the aspirant to discipleship.

The fourth and final stage of the meditation is intended to gather up and direct the effects of sustained "reflection" or contemplation, on the work of preparation for the Christ's reappearance: "Consider practically what you can do in the coming week to further the preparation for the coming of the Christ."

It is significant here that the attention is directed in meditation not to any long-range planning but to the possibilities of "the coming week", seven short days. Obviously the three phases of the work already done in meditation should have an increasingly powerful effect in the consciousness of those so working; attitudes of mind and heart should become increasingly transmuted, purified, redeemed, enlightened and loving. The will-to-good of the divine Purpose should become increasingly dominant, superseding the little personal will. So each meditator contributes to the whole process of redemption within the planet and cooperates with the necessary task of "preparing men's minds and hearts" for the emergence of the Christ. Each week that passes and with every use of the special meditation, these effects should be apparent. But what more can be done?

"Consider *practically*" what can be done in the days ahead. What opportunities are there to awaken more people to the fact of the Christ's coming? What opportunities can be *created?* How can the Great Invocation be introduced to more people in more languages? How can the *hindrances* to the reappearance of the Christ be swept away?

The "hindrances" are said to be two: first, "the inertia of the average spiritually-minded men and women;" and second, "lack of financial support for the work of the Christ." These two could well supply for most a fruitful field for service on a day to day, week to week, basis.

Inertia? Do we start with ourselves? What prevents us from taking a more active part in the work of preparation? Is it inertia, or fear, or do we justify both by calling them "prudence," necessary caution in expressing potentially explosive or unacceptable ideas? What could be more potent, more dynamic, more evocative, than the personal example of intelligent, enthusiastic and persistent activity devoted to the work of preparation for the Coming One?

And *money?* The lack of money for today's work of preparation for the reappearance of the Christ is the motive behind the second redemptive meditation which the Tibetan Master has asked us all to use on

Sunday every week, taking what we have ourselves *saved* during the week and dedicating it, in meditation, to the work of the Christ; for if we do not give, we may not ask.

This meditation is said to be "so simple that many of you may regard it as innocuous and perhaps futile. Used by many simultaneously, it may shatter the impasse which at present prevents adequate funds pouring into the work which the Hierarchy seeks to accomplish." Here again we can see the potency generated by many minds working together in unity of purpose, minds capable of translating idea and ideal into practical action.

We are asked also to "Realise the occult Law that 'to those who give shall be given' so that they can give again. . . . Attempt to feel true love sweeping through you and have the fixed intention to express this love to all you contact. It is the great attractive and selfless agent in world affairs." The view is held by some that if one is working for true "spiritual" goals then the money needed will automatically flow into the work without any special attention being given to it and, certainly, without the need for a special meditation. This is no doubt true for those who have achieved a *perfect* soul alignment, a completed ability to work at all times "according to occult law" and with a constant and undeviating demonstration of "true love." But this would mean, working as a member of the Hierarchy where such a spiritual status exists; whereas, we are still involved in the imperfections and limitations of the human centre and, with those limitations, still carry a definite responsibility for helping to release the needed vast sums of money for the work of preparation for the coming of the Christ. Therefore, we can achieve that goal by aligning ourselves in meditation with the spiritual Laws and Principles and the dynamic and attractive energies which, alone, will bring about a regeneration of that crystallised energy we call money.

We are working, during this period of preparation and transition, in the most difficult period in world history; at a time when the forces of materialism have become entrenched and over-influential at the concrete level of human living. Releasing this crystallised money energy from the channels in which it now flows and from the selfish purposes which it now so largely serves is a task in which only the "pure in heart" can effectively participate. By "pure in heart," I mean selfless, spiritually motivated, loving and giving, intelligently active on behalf of the Plan, aware of the desperate needs of the human family and committed to service. In this framework, the meditation goes forward.

Most of the work required is done through visualisation: visualising the present materialistic focus of money energy; the stream of flowing golden substance or energy, which money can become through right attitudes of mind and heart, passing into the "control of the Forces of Light"; visualising the work to be done by those groups and individuals who are attempting to cooperate with the hierarchical Plan; and then, through the "creative imagination and by an act of the will, see untold and unlimited sums of money pouring into the hands of those who seek to do the Masters' work." This is the magical and critical part of the whole meditation; it is this imaginative and will-full direction of money energy—knowing full well that *energy does follow thought*—which tends eventually to release the crystallised hold of self-centred minds and hearts, bit by bit, one or two or three at a time. Money energy is thereby lifted, cleansed, redeemed and used for the purposes of working out the Plan. Money once directed into spiritual channels, can never again revert to its previous state, or be held hostage by human materialism and selfishness. Redemption is a one-time, for-all-time, act of renewal and restoration.

In meditation, we say, with conviction and emphasis: "He for whom the whole world waits has said that whatsoever shall be asked in his name and with faith in the response will see it accomplished," and we add, "I ask for the needed money (for the work) and can demand it because . . . From the centre which we call the race of men let the Plan of Love and Light work out and may it seal the door where evil dwells."

The regular use of these redemptive meditations is therefore a superlative way we can cooperate *every week* in the work of preparing human consciousness, the minds and hearts of humanity, for the imminent reappearance of the Christ. Effective work requires all that we have to give, mentally, as souls and servers, aligned with the planetary heart and the divine Will; and all the creative intelligent service of which we are capable.

The esoteric group in the world has been created to serve every form of planetary need and in any planetary emergency. We are today working within the greatest spiritual crisis point of human history and at a time of planetary reorientation. We can "dedicate ourselves anew" to the work of the Christ, with "no other life intention" in confident knowledge that as we do so we are in alignment with the constructive, irresistible powers of Life itself, that Light and Love and Purpose which alone can restore the Plan on Earth.

CHAPTER 5 (I)—According to Law

The laws under which this solar system of ours is governed, are expressions of God's quality and character. We live in an orderly universe; there is rhythm, ebb and flow, law and order, to all things under the sun. Only man, on planet Earth, endowed with self-will and entrusted with the willing transformation of his unregenerate material substance, sets up a counter rhythm, an irritant in the smooth meshing of cosmic cycles. It seems that at one vital point in the evolutionary process many aeons ago, mankind established a life rhythm contrary to that flowing and circulating throughout the universe. This may have been due to failure to respond adequately to energy stimulation and to the attainable goals in that particular period. For whatever cause, however, in astrological terms mankind reversed his passage around the wheel of life, the zodiac. He became inturned on himself, creating a self-centred separateness going against the current of the divine circulatory flow. This reversal continues to dominate the individual man, selfishly controlled until he achieves the necessary reorientation in consciousness. This reorientation transforms the self-centred, self-serving individual into the decentralised server of humanity, and re-establishes the life rhythm within the zodiac in a counter-clockwise direction in conformity with the cosmic procedure.

All this long process is regulated by law, cosmic, systemic and the laws in the three worlds. Man is at all times susceptible to the working of these laws, no matter how reactionary his attitudes may be, or how antagonistic to divine law and his own political, legislative and legal practices and institutions. He is swayed by influences and energies of which he knows nothing throughout a long period of time while the animal man in him struggles to maintain its supremacy in the face of perpetual energy impacts modified by cosmic, systemic and natural law.

There is one basic law called the Law of Periodicity, which governs all manifestation. This differentiates into three fundamental cosmic laws and seven systemic laws, all with numerous subsidiary laws operating at different levels of consciousness The three cosmic laws are well known: the Law of Synthesis governing spirit (or life), the Law of Attraction governing soul (or consciousness), the Law of Economy governing matter (or form). All lesser laws relate to these three underlying energy influences expressing the major divine aspects—the Will aspect, first ray energy; the Love aspect, second ray energy; and the Activity aspect, third ray energy.

Between the three cosmic laws and their differentiation into the seven systemic laws exists an intermediate law. This is the synthetic law of the system of Sirius, with which our planet Earth is so closely linked. While the Sirian system and our solar system function through independent internal economies, causes rising in Sirius affect our system under the Law of Karma because of the correspondences existing between the systemic Lords of Karma and the Lord on Sirius. The Sirian Law of Karma, therefore, is intermediate between the three cosmic and the seven systemic laws reminding us of the effects on planet Earth of the ancient relationship existing between the Lord of Sirius and our planetary Logos. The effect of this ancient relationship brings into the forefront the Principle of Freedom as it creates a "pathway of power" between Sirius and the spiritual Hierarchy on planet Earth. The Law of Karma, and the Principle of Freedom are correlatives. Freedom and liberation result from careful observance of the Law of Karma leading to its ultimate transcendence.

Where the solar system is concerned and the effects on the solar Logos, it seems that this Sirian Law of Karma controls His actions in much the same way as the soul eventually controls the evolving human personality. The higher we go, the further out into the living space of the universe, the more we realise that relationships within the cosmos are reflected throughout all forms of manifestation, from the solar system to a planet, to a kingdom in nature, to a man. Each one of us in due process of evolution forms part of one of the Heavenly Men, Who Themselves form the energy centers within that greater Heavenly Man, the solar Logos, Who forms part of the consciousness of the Logos of Sirius. In His turn, the Sirian Logos forms one of the seven Grand Heavenly Men, the centres in the body of the "One About Whom Naught May Be Said." This is the great Being who "gives sustenance to the universe."

There's a basic truth in the realisation that the Laws under which the solar system of ours is governed, are expressions of God's quality and character. Similarly, mankind reveals his own quality and character in the Laws and Principles he adopts as a controlling influence in his life. How do the great Laws, the one, the three, and the seven, affect the lives of the race of man? How do we respond? For in response is revealed the extent to which the soul is in control of the evolving personality. The one basic Law, the law of Periodicity, is based upon the rhythmic beat of the central heart, or sun, of any organism from a universe to an individual egoic life. It is the originating impulse leading to cyclic manifestation in form. The Law of Periodicity involves cyclic repetition in space, in time, in form and through the note sounded on different planes and subplanes. The Laws of Karma and of Rebirth are inevitably linked to the Law of Periodicity. The soul in man ever seeks, through repeated incarnations, for a perfecting of that experience which will liberate from the wheel of rebirth.

Neglected opportunities are re-presented, experiences are repeated, until the needed lessons are learned affecting the state of consciousness and the quality of the manifested life. Today we see clearly the urgent need for human life and human institutions to reflect the great spiritual Laws which lie behind the evolutionary cycles.

The initiation of the race into the mystery of the ages, now in process, is due to the first stirring of human response to the Will of God. It is the Will of God to produce certain radical and momentous changes in the consciousness of the race which will completely alter man's attitude to life. The Law of Synthesis, controlling the Will aspect of deity, is a stimulating influence of great potency affecting the field of government. The selfishness of the little minds in the various legislatures of the world, must in some way be offset. That is the problem. The minds of men are, however, responding to this most potent energy accessible to humanity. Human attitudes and human thinking *are* changing.

The production of unity and synthesis in all human relations is becoming more important to more people and even to some national governments. The forming of the United Nations is a result of this growing tendency towards a practical union within the world community of men. The opening of human hearts and minds to cosmic and spiritual Law depends primarily, during this solar cycle, on response to the second great cosmic law, the Law of Attraction. In a cosmic sense, this corresponds to the systemic Law of Love. The compelling attraction of this energy dominating the second solar system holds all elements within the system in magnetic and orderly relationship, the planets revolving around their central nucleus, the sun, and lesser atomic and molecular matter circulating around a magnetic centre within the planet and within all material forms. Through this magnetic power, all things are held within the circle of divine love. All hearts and minds are subject to its influence. For the first time in history there is today definite world action which reflects the many qualities of love; compassion, inclusiveness, concern, a reaching out to help and to alleviate suffering and deprivation and to provide wise and practical means for self help.

These efforts to share and cooperate, impulsed by love and based on the sense of oneness and unity, also relate to the third cosmic Law of Economy. The Law of Economy adjusts all that concerns the material and spiritual evolution of the cosmos to the best possible advantage and with the least expenditure of force. It makes perfect each atom of time and each eternal period, and carries all onward and upward, and through, with the least possible effort, with the proper adjustment of equilibrium and with the necessary rate of rhythm. We need to ponder on this for it holds the secret of peace. Surely these words can be applied to the desperate need for peace in today's world. Stability, harmony, right relationship and world peace depend on the right and rhythmic use of all energy and resources, with the least expenditure of force, directed towards all areas of need. Right distribution based on the principle of sharing, requires an intelligent establishing of priorities and a wise understanding that the resources of the world belong to mankind, as the race of men, responsible for maintaining the balance of nature on which the subhuman kingdoms as well as the human depend. Maintaining right balance and give and take within the environment of planet Earth, is a charge on the human kingdom linking superhuman and subhuman states of awareness.

Within the three basic cosmic Laws, the seven Laws of the solar system affect the seven planes on planet Earth. We have the Law of Vibration: all is fire or energy. The Law of Cohesion: that which produces coalescence or magnetic attraction. The Law of Disintegration: the rejection of the matter of the various sheaths, the bodies, as the spiritual being achieves liberation, The Law of Magnetic Control by which the Monad controls the personality via the soul, The Law of Fixation: mental control and stimulation, producing coherency. The Law of Love: transmuting the desire nature through the magnetic love of the buddhic plane. And the Law of Sacrifice and Death controlling the physical plane, the destruction of the form that evolving life may progress.

These final three Laws, of Fixation, of Love, and of Sacrifice and Death, tend to dominate the human being as the laws of the three worlds, affecting his mental, emotional, and physical states of consciousness. Through them he achieves purification, renunciation and initiation into the consciousness aspect of our planetary Life, the spiritual Hierarchy, the fifth kingdom in nature and the first superhuman planetary centre. While response is unconscious for long ages of time, growth and awareness from the animal man to the spiritual being proceeds, governed and regulated by the Laws and the energies which constantly impact the states of consciousness and life in which we are immersed. Gradually, man achieves mastery within the spiritual and cosmic Laws and on the ray energies. His environment feels the effects of his increasing sphere of radiation. The light he generates and transmits lifts and lightens the way for others.

The whole process of response to Law is due now to be speeded up for Libra is "the sponsor of the Law" and the influence of Libra is destined to assume "a position of power in the planetary horoscope" towards the end of this century. This might imply that humanity is beginning to identify the laws of the three worlds and to find them good; that he is dimly responding to the seven laws of the solar system, finding them present in the substance and planes of his consciousness with its form-building propensities, that he instinctively determines and chooses his way in conformity with the three cosmic Laws.

The objective of the evolutionary process which involves all forms of life on our planet is to develop a sensitivity which makes revelation possible. Revelation is the goal of all experience, each revelation carrying the initiate closer to the Heart of the Sun wherein all things are known and felt and through which all forms, all beings, and all things, can be bathed in love. It is part of our planetary purpose, under the influence of solar purpose, to liberate light and love into a wider universe and to free the solar system from the attacks of cosmic evil.

The quality of Love-Wisdom, which animates our planetary Logos and is the basic quality of the entire solar system, is revealed in those who attain liberation and resurrection upon our planet. Such initiates are always qualified by divine love, and divine love will also be the underlying quality of all they may later create when freed from our planet. It is quite clear, therefore, why the phrase "God is love" is in reality our planetary keynote demonstration, under the Law, of God's quality and character. It is the will of God that all men love and serve one another. In these few words are summed up the direct power of the three great Laws of Synthesis, of Attraction, and of Economy to which, at long last, the race of men is opening both mind and heart.

CHAPTER 5 (II)—The Way of Liberation

Love-Wisdom is the primary energy of this second solar system, and the Law of Attraction is the dominant Law. The Christ taught and exemplified a new concept in line with this primary energy and Law; the concept of a loving and compassionate God—*God is Love*. Therefore, it is the basic underlying purpose of every incarnating soul on this planet to manifest, eventually, a totally selfless love. "Asking nothing and expecting nothing for the separated self," such a love, unconsciously radiated or consciously given to others, enhances the process of liberation from form control.

Only a purely selfless love has that liberating effect. It liberates the person who achieves it from the prison of himself; and it affects the as yet untransmuted planetary substance. Individual human beings, the human family as a whole, and the manifested planetary Life, all find liberation and freedom by the same means.

Christianity through the ages has extolled the power of love as "the greatest thing in the world." But the selfless aspects of giving love are seldom emphasised, except in the most general terms, although it is this quality of love which approximates and reflects the Christ's example. And today, at world crisis point, such a love can begin to manifest when it is most needed through those who have been willing to accept the demands and difficulties of utter self-forgetfulness.

Through the process of evolution, rebirth, experience, and growth, mankind will eventually achieve liberation from the material aspects of life on this planet and from the wheel of rebirth. Such an exhilarating prospect can stimulate the conscious choice needed to love, without thought of self, to give for the joy of giving, without personal considerations of convenience, time or place. To love is to serve. And service is "the right use of energy to meet a recognised need on any level of consciousness." Love and service support and complement one another; but for transformation and transcendence of the personality and liberation of the soul, the life within the form, the voice of the little self must be totally silent.

"Selfless love," simple, familiar, and relatively meaningless words for long ages. But they hold the key to planetary redemption.

Five centuries or so before the Christ, the Buddha taught in almost the same terms. He said to His Bhikshus, "The greatest of all is the loving heart. . . . All methods for the earning of merit in this life are not worth one sixteenth part of love, the deliverance of mind. Love, the deliverance of mind, takes them all into itself, shining and glowing and beaming."

Love, the deliverance of mind. Here is the essential fusion of heart and mind, a fusion which liberates man from himself, releasing him into the fullness of life on Earth, planetary cooperation, and co-creation with God.

The same thought is revealed in what is said to be the major task of the new group of world servers—"to reveal the soul of the nations." Whatever may be the type of energy inspiring the soul aspect of the many nations of the world—and it covers the whole seven-note range—basic to the soul principle (the second in every triplicity) in every nation as in every individual human being, is the energy and the power of love. The task of revealing that love in all relationships and all aspects of daily life demands liberation, liberation from self-interest and self-will in those individuals and groups carrying responsibility for human progress and well being. Right human relations can only be established on such a basis, and the ultimate of right human relationships is world peace.

To reveal the soul of one's own nation, therefore, means to think with love., and to act with goodwill no matter what the circumstances, for goodwill *is* "love in action." Such attributes are revelatory of the soul and attract the soul's attention.

A similar, or parallel, meaning can be found in all the keynotes for the disciple relating to the twelve signs of the zodiac. The twelve keynotes form an unbroken and evolving circle, each one developing from one neighbour and extending into the next, no matter where one breaks into the circle.

It seems that the keynote for Libra is of particular significance at this period of the twentieth century, and it also holds the key to liberation through self-less love: "I choose the way which leads between the two great lines of force." One might ask, why choose the unattached, the "way between." Why not the way of the soul, the way of life, which would seem to be more natural to the disciple? And perhaps it is, or would be unless the disciple is a "real" one and, there-fore, liberated within himself and focussed upon the purposes and plans of planetary evolution.

At this point in the evolution of the planet and all its kingdoms in nature, it is the function of the human kingdom, the fourth, to act as the relating factor between the sub-human and the super-human king-doms. Through a humanity which is both spiritual and material in substance, the "higher" and "lower" kingdoms will achieve reconciliation. Or, to put it another way, the essential service of the human cen-tre is to *manifest* the fusion of spirit and matter and to evolve out of the two the third, the middle way, the transcendent path of the soul in which the life aspect (spirit) is alive and dominant, and the matter aspect (form) irradiated and transfigured, so providing oppor-tunities for creating a way of life on Earth, closer to the attainable, if relative, perfection of the Life "in Whom we live and move and have our being."

It is also significant that in this keynote we see the essential value of free choice. We *choose* to cooperate with the purposes of our planetary life, as well as we can understand and interpret them, by creating the path of reconciliation (the antahkarana in an individual), bringing together in right relationship the ultimate pairs of opposites—spirit and matter, energy and force. First comes a personal reconciliation and liberation, and then, by a joyous sense of identification with all that lives and breathes, the larger purpose can be served. We stand between "the two great lines of force," involutionary and evolutionary, a part of both, attached to neither, free to relate and reconcile the apparently separated and irreconcilable. This is the path of conscious return; this is selfless love at its most potent. And it leads from "I God, I matter am", (Virgo) to the triumphant emergence of the warrior disciple from the battlefields of his own state of consciousness (Scorpio).

Simply put, selfless love is conformity to God's will; selfless love is identification with the mind and the heart of the Christ in us, "the hope of glory;" selfless love is aware of human need and going out to meet it; selfless love is the daily service rendered in the little things and circumstances involving those around us; selfless love is response to the voice of the life force as it extends through all things and all beings in all kingdoms of nature. Selfless love is the way of liberation for all.

CHAPTER 6—Atomic Energy—Curse or Blessing?

The recent nuclear plant disaster in Chernobyl, near Kiev in the Soviet Union, has given fuel to the anti-nuclear movement and once again raised questions for many about the future, if any, of this form of energy for industrial and domestic use. In this context it is illuminating to re-read the chapter on "The Release of Atomic Energy," written in August 1945, published in the book, *The Externalisation of the Hierarchy* by Alice Bailey, pp. 491-500. Much of that brief text is given here as the basis for a little further thought on the whole matter of the real significance of such an energy "release" at such an historic moment in planetary—not merely human—evolution when the Forces of Light and the Forces of Evil were locked in struggle.

Here are the most important passages from that chapter:

"I would like at this time to touch upon the greatest spiritual event which has taken place since the fourth kingdom of nature, the human kingdom, appeared. I refer to the release of atomic energy . . . in connection with the bombing of Japan.

Some years ago I told you that the new era would be ushered in by the scientists of the world and that the inauguration of the kingdom of God on Earth would be heralded by means of successful scientific investigation. By this first step in the releasing of the energy of the atom, this has been accomplished, . . . Let me make one or two statements about this discovery, leaving you to make your own application and deductions. Little as to the true nature of this happening is as yet known, and still less is understood. Certain ideas and suggested thoughts may be of real value here and enable you to see this stupendous event in better perspective.

1. It was the imminence of this 'release' of energy which was one of the major subjective factors in the precipitation of this last phase of the war. This world war started in 1914, but its last and most important phase began in 1939. Up till then it was a world war. After that date, and because the forces of evil took advantage of the state of war and belligerency existing on the planet, the real war began, involving the entire three worlds of human evolution and a consequent activity of the Hierarchy. Man's attention is normally focussed on the exterlities of living. Nevertheless, all great discoveries, such as those made in connection with astronomy or in relation to the laws of nature or involving such a revelation as that of radio-activity, or the epoch-making event announced this week concerning the first steps taken in the harnessing of cosmic energy, are ever the result of inner pressure emanating from Forces and Lives found in high Places. Such inner pressures themselves function under the laws of the Spirit and not just under what you call natural laws; they are the result of the impelling work of certain great Lives, working in connection with the third aspect of divinity, that of active intelligence, and are concerned with the substance or matter aspect of manifestation. Such activities are motivated from Shamballa. This activity is set in motion by these Lives, working on Their high plane, and it gradually causes a reaction in the various departments of the Hierarchy, particularly those working under third, fifth and seventh ray Masters. Eventually, disciples upon the physical levels of activity become aware of the inner ferment, and this happens either consciously or unconiously. They become 'impressed,' and sci-

entific work is then started and carried through into the stages of experimentation and final success.

One point should here be remembered, and that is that this phase applies to both the great White Lodge and the Black Lodge—the one dedicated to the beneficent task of purifying and aiding all lives in the three worlds of material evolution and to the release of the soul in form, and the other to the retardation of the evolutionary process and to the continuous crystallising of material forms which hide and veil the *anima mundi*. Both groups have been profoundly interested and implicated in this matter of the release of energy from the atom and the liberation of its inner aspect, but their motives and objectives were widely different.

2. The imminence of this release—inevitably and under direction—produced an enormous tension in hierarchical circles because (to express the idea colloquially) a race was on between the Dark Forces and the Forces of Light to acquire possession of the techniques necessary to bring about this liberation of needed energy. Had the Dark Forces triumphed, and had the Axis Powers obtained possession of the needed scientific formulas, it would have led to a major planetary disaster. The released energy would have been used first of all to bring about the complete destruction of all opposing the forces of evil, and then it would have been prostituted to the preservation of an increasingly materialistic and non-idealistic civilisation. Germany could not be trusted with this power, for all her motives were compellingly wrong.

You might here fall back on the trite religious platitude that the innate good in humanity and mankind's inherent divinity would eventually have triumphed, because naught can finally overcome the universal trend to good. You are prone to forget that if the evil forces possess potencies which

can destroy form in the three worlds on such a wide
scale that the souls of advanced aspirants and disciples, and those of initiates seeking incarnation,
cannot come into outer expression during a particular world crisis, then you have direfully affected
the time-schedule of the evolutionary process; you
will have greatly delayed (perhaps for millenia of
years) the manifestation of the kingdom of God.
The time had come for that manifestation, and
hence the powerful activity of the dark forces.

This attempt to hinder the planned progress con-
stituted a definite menace and indicated a supreme
danger and problem. The evil forces were closer to
success than any of you have dreamed. They were
so close to success in 1942 that there were four
months when the members of the spiritual Hierarchy had made every possible arrangement to withdraw from human contact for an indefinite and
unforeseen period of time; the plans for a closer
contact with the evolutionary process in the three
worlds and the effort to blend and fuse the two
divine centres, the Hierarchy and humanity, into
one working collaborating whole seemed doomed
to destruction. Their fusion would have meant the
appearance of the Kingdom of God on Earth; the
obstacles to this fusion, owing to the active tension of the dark forces, seemed at that time insuperable; we believed that man would go down to
defeat, owing to his selfishness and his misuse of
the principle of free will. We made all preparations
to withdraw, and yet at the same time we strug-
gled to get humanity to choose rightly and to see
the issues clearly.

The necessity to withdraw was averted. I may
not say in what manner, beyond telling you that
the Lords of Liberation took certain unexpected
steps. This They were led to do owing to the invocative powers of humanity, used consciously by all

those upon the side of the will-to-good and unconsciously by all men of goodwill. Owing to these steps, the efforts of those fighting in the realm of science for the establishing of true knowledge and right human relations were aided. The trend of the power to know and to discover (a definite form of energy) was *deflected away* from the demanding evocative minds of those seeking to destroy the world of men, leading to a form of mental paralysis. Those seeking to emphasise the right values and to save humanity were simultaneously stimulated to the point of success.

In these very few words I have disposed of a stupendous world event. and in this brief paragraph I have summed up the working out of a specialised divine activity. (My italics. M.B.)

3. When the sun moved northward that year (1942), the great White Lodge knew that the battle had been won. Their preparations were halted and the Masters then organised for renewed effort (through Their disciples) to bring about those conditions wherein that which was new and that which was in line with loving divine purpose could freely move forward. The war was not won by the surrender of Germany. That was only the outer result of inner happenings. The war was won by the Forces of Light when the mental potency of the forces of evil was overcome and the 'energy of the future' was directed or impelled by Those Who were seeking the higher human values and the spiritual good of mankind. Four factors lie behind the momentous happening of the release of this form of atomic energy, through the medium of what is erroneously and unscientifically called the 'splitting of the atom.' There are other factors, but you may find the following four of real interest:

a. There was a clearly directed inflow of extra-planetary energy released by the Lords of Liberation, to Whom invocation had been successfully made; through the impact of this energy upon the atomic substance being dealt with by the investigating scientists, changes were brought about which enabled them to achieve success. The experiments being carried forward were therefore both subjective and objective.

b. A concerted effort was made by a number of disciples who were working in fifth and seventh ray ashrams, and this enabled them to impress lesser disciples in the scientific field and helped them to surmount the well-nigh insuperable difficulties with which they were confronted.

c. There was also a weakening of the tension which had hitherto successfully held the forces of evil together, and a growing inability of the evil group at the head of the Axis Powers to surmount the incidental war fatigue. This brought about, first of all, a steady deterioration of their minds, and then of their brains and nervous systems. None of the men involved in the direction of the Axis effort in Europe is today normal psychologically; they are all suffering from some form of physical deterioration, and this has been a real factor in their defeat, though one that may be difficult for you to realise. It is not so in the case of the Japanese, whose psychological make-up is totally different, as are their nervous systems, which are of fourth rootrace quality. They will be and are being defeated by physical war measures and by the destruction physically of their war potential and the death of the form aspect. *This destruction . . . and the consequent release of their imprisoned souls, is a necessary happening; it is the justification of the use of the atomic bomb upon the Japanese population. The first use of this released energy has been destructive, but I would remind you that it has*

been the destruction of forms and not the destruc-
tion of spiritual values and the death of the human
spirit — as was the goal of the Axis effort. (My
italics. M.B.)

Forget not that all success (both good and bad)
is dependent upon the sustaining of the point
of tension. This point of tension involves the
dynamic focussing of all mental, emotional and
physical energies at a central point of planned
activity. This, by the way, is the objective of all
true meditation work. It is in this act of tension
that the German people failed. This cost them
the war; their tension broke because the group
of evil forces who were impressing the negative
German people were unable to attain the point
of tension which the Hierarchy could reach when
it was reinforced through the action of the Lords
of Liberation.

d. Another factor was the constant, invocative
demand and the prayers (articulate and inarticu-
late) of humanity itself. Man, impelled largely
by fear and the innate mobilising of the human
spirit against slavery, reached such a pitch of
demanding energy that a channel was created
which greatly facilitated the work of the Hierarchy, under the direct influence of the Lords of
Liberation.

4. The release of the energy of the atom is as yet
in an extremely embryonic stage; humanity little
knows the extent or the nature of the energies which
have been tapped and released. There are many
types of atoms, constituting the 'world substance';
each can release its own type of force; this is one of
the secrets which the new age will in time reveal,
but a good and sound beginning has been made. I
would call your attention to the words, 'the liberation of energy.' It is *liberation* which is the keynote
of the spiritually oriented aspirant. This liberation

has started by the release of an aspect of matter *and the freeing of some of the soul forces within the atom. This has been. for matter itself, a great and potent initiation, paralleling those initiations which liberate or release the souls of men.* (My italics. M.B.)

In this process of planetary initiation humanity has carried its work as the world saviour down into the world of substance, and has affected those primary units of life of which all forms are made. (My italics. M.B.)

5. You will now understand the meaning of the words used by so many of you in the second of the Great Invocations: *The hour of service of the saving force has now arrived.* This 'saving force' is the energy which science has released into the world for the destruction, first of all, of those who continue (if they do) to defy the Forces of Light working through the United Nations. (It seems clear that the Allied forces are meant here, not the world organisation. M.B.) Then—as time goes on—*this liberated energy will usher in the new civilisation, the new and better world and the finer, more spiritual conditions.* (My italics. M.B.) The highest dreams of those who love their fellowmen can become practical possibilities through the right use of this liberated energy, *if the real values are taught, emphasised and applied to daily living. . . .* (My italics. M.B.)

. . . the first use of this energy has been material destruction; this was inevitable and desirable; old forms (obstructing the good) have had to be destroyed; the wrecking and disappearance of that which is bad and undesirable must ever precede the building of the good and desirable and the longed-for emergence of that which is new and better.

The constructive use of this energy and its harnessing for the betterment of humanity is its real

purpose; this living energy of substance itself, hitherto shut up within the atom and imprisoned in these
ultimate forms of life, can be turned wholly into that
which is good and can bring about such a revolution-
ising of the modes of human experience that (from
one angle alone) it will necessitate and bring about
an entirely new economic world structure.

It lies in the hands of the United Nations to pro-
tect this released energy from misuse and to see
that its power is not prostituted to selfish ends
and purely material purposes. It is a 'saving force'
and has in it the potency of rebuilding, of rehabili-
tation and of reconstruction. Its right use can abol-
ish destitution, bring civilised comfort (and not
useless luxury) to all upon our planet; its expression in forms of right living, if motivated by right
human relations, will produce beauty, warmth,
colour, the abolition of the present forms of disease, the withdrawal of mankind from all its activities which involve living or working underground,
and will bring to an end all human slavery, all need
to work or fight for possessions and things, and
will render possible a state of life which will leave
man free to pursue the higher aims of the spirit.
The prostituting of life to the task of providing the
bare necessities or to making it possible for a few
rich and privileged people to have too much when
others have too little, will come to an end; men
everywhere can now be released into a state of life
which will give them leisure and time to follow spiritual objectives, to realise richer cultural life, and
to attain a broader mental perspective.

But, my brothers, men will fight to prevent this;
the reactionary groups in every country will neither recognise the need for, nor desire this new
world order ... the vested interests, the big car-
tels, trusts and monopolies that controlled the past
few decades, preceding this world war, will mobi-

lise their resources and fight to the death to prevent the extinction of their sources of income. . . .
Signs of this opposition can already be seen. . . .
World decisions must therefore, in the future, be
based upon a steady determination to further right
human relations, and to prevent selfish control,
financial or ecclesiastical, by any group of men, any-
where, in any country. . . . The future of the world
lies in the hands of the men of goodwill and in those
who have unselfish purpose everywhere." (*The Externalisation of the Hierarchy*, pp. 491-500).

From these words it is clear that, from the hierarchical perspective, the work of the scientists which
ultimately produced the atomic bomb was influenced
by profound subjective stimulation, causing the "greatest spiritual event which has taken place since the
fourth kingdom in nature, the human kingdom, appeared," and that this event "ushered in the new era
and the inauguration of the kingdom of God on Earth."

Reading those words in the light of what humanity
has done, by conscious and deliberate choice, with
this powerful energy since, in the form of bombs, it
was used to bring to an end the final stage of World
War II in Japan, one might well question their accuracy and the "humaneness" of the attitude of mind
which could evaluate atomic energy as a "saving force"
and a means of liberation for a form-centred humanity, trapped in selfish materialism. And many who
study the teachings of the Tibetan and have read these
passages, do question their validity and are troubled
and confused by statements which appear to contra-
dict the experience we have had with the development of nuclear energy since the doors were opened.

Indeed, our experience has been so drastic and so
potentially lethal to the human race—and to life on
this planet—that an active anti-nuclear movement has
grown up across the world which would ban not only
nuclear weapons but any form of nuclear-powered

energy for any use whatsoever. And this poses a further problem for those whose vision of a liberating force for the human race, when correctly developed and used, is inspired, knowingly or unknowingly, by a subjective reality.

It seems that in this emergent new force for good, which depends upon human intelligence and integrity for right development, we have acted with typical blindness and selfishness, and with apathy. We always seem to go off first in the wrong direction, creating problems and hazards, before we are willing to reconsider our basic aims and adhere to an ideal purpose. Governed as we are by the fourth ray energy of harmony through conflict, we have an ingrained tendency to swing from one extreme to the other before eventually establishing a balance and harmony in line with the right way ahead according to Plan.

In this case, however, which is a highly technical and scientific issue, linked to national and international policies and politics, we have been pulled in the wrong direction by greed, fear, and blatant self-interest. Perpetuation of the fear of any political system or way of life different from our own and, therefore, threatening to national sovereignty, has led in this century to what President Eisenhower called the "industrial-military complex." This powerful force, existing in most of the major countries of the world, benefits from a continuing military build-up, whether we call it "defence," "offence," or "preparedness." And this power has over-influenced and out-voted those who see the potential benefits of an atomic power devoted to human welfare. As a result, due also to the nuclear waste disposal dilemma, we have placed this planet in jeopardy for thousands of years.

And yet there are ways this force can be safely, harmlessly and cheaply developed. Consider the two known methods of creating this energy — nuclear *fission* and nuclear *fusion*. Fission is the present method of production, dangerous, and of long-range radiatory effect. Fusion is the method many are fighting to develop, fighting for funds, for recognition and for support. The fusion method is safe, clear and cheap, using an abundant source of fuel—the hydrogen element in water. One only has to consider the meaning of the two words—fission and fusion—to realise which one is in line with hierarchical intent; *fusion* is part of the philosophy of Hierarchy.

The August (1986) conference in Vienna attended by nuclear scientists from all over the world to consider the international implications of the Chernobyl accident, concluded that this was due entirely to human error—error in the design and construction of the reactor; and error in its operation.

They also concluded, however, that the peoples of the world need, and must have, the benefits of nuclear power for its future energy requirements This means that a safe method of producing nuclear energy which will not threaten or endanger life on Earth either now or for future generations, *must* be found. And we know this can be done if adequate research and development resources are made available. It means that the *greed* of a few, which now dominates and exploits the nuclear industry, must be replaced by the *need* of the many—humanity as a whole. And this, of course, is involved in the major change in consciousness humanity faces today. We are at a turning point in history, a time when humanity is capable of taking a giant step forward in consciousness. The soul *must* more adequately "control the outer form, and life, and all events," and that is the responsibility of all of us, exercising an influence on all aspects of human life on Earth.

It seems inevitable that, at this stage in its planetary evolution, humanity should be more aware of the destruction of form resulting from the use of two atomic bombs than with the liberation of the soul within the form. But this liberation and new opportunity, to the spiritual Hierarchy, is the real consequence of the bombs and their only justification because here the evolution of rootraces (and subraces) is concerned, with far-reaching implications

Far more depends upon our present decisions on the future of atomic energy than appears on the surface. This crisis is concerned not merely with a source of energy for human use—at present largely monopolised by military demands—but it represents an opportunity to respond in a new way to the influence of the soul and to listen to the voice of Hierarchy. We can now, if we choose, better manifest the soul's presence in us by reasserting the spiritual values and standards which should govern our daily lives, and by demanding that national policies and international relationships be controlled by them. No one of us can evade this personal responsibility for the future of the world. And those few whose vision is beginning to approximate that of the Hierarchy and the Plan for humanity, carry a particular responsibility. This is what discipleship represents. The responsibility of knowledge; the responsibility of love and service; and the responsibility of manifesting the vision and the Plan of Hierarchy and the Christ.

CHAPTER 7—The New Psychology is in the Making!*

Psychology, I suppose, is a relatively new science which interests many of us today. And a new psychology is in the making because we are beginning to understand it as an integral part of the whole structure of modern society, rather than as an isolated, or separate, science.

Although we are supposed to be living in an age of specialisation, these days it seems almost impossible to detect exactly when or where certain of the sciences begin to merge into one another. When does psychology become philosophy, and philosophy theology, and theology ethics and patterns of behaviour, for example? There is a great deal to be said for moving away from the over-specialisation of the immediate past, which has limited knowledge, and understanding and capacity. The British magazine, *Punch*, a year or two ago published a cartoon showing two surgeons leaving the operating theatre, removing their masks and gowns, with one saying to the other, "That was too close for comfort. Another eighth of an inch, and I'd have been out of my field!"

There is an esoteric aphorism which suggests that the path of wisdom lies in working "from the universal to the particular," from the whole to the part. And this attitude of mind—or consciousness—is entirely characteristic of the twenty-four books written by Alice A. Bailey over a thirty-year period. These books are intended to help prepare for—to precede and condition—the new age. We are moving into a new

---

* Talk prepared for the Psychology Society, Baruch College of the City University of New York, April 16, 1981.

age, recognised and welcomed by many people and groups today around the world, and covering the whole spectrum of human life and experience. And this is an astronomical fact, not a figment of an over-stimulated or mystical imagination. Within the cyclic movements and relationships within our universe, the sun is now moving into a fairly long period of contact and relationship with the constellation Aquarius. Whether or not we can agree that this brings in new and different energies and opportunities, we will all agree that this brings need for change in the way people and nations interact with one another, and organise their own political, economic and social ways of living. We are facing the need for change every-where, in every way; and we are living through a transition period between one age and another when opportunities for change are becoming increasingly apparent—and urgent—with every day that passes. Because of the destructive power acquired by human-ity during the course of this century, change has become imperative for human survival.

Change: John Henry, Cardinal Newman, is reported to have said that "in higher worlds it may be other-wise, but here below, to live is to change, and to be perfect, is to have changed often!" So we are talking about changes in consciousness; changes in human attitudes of mind and heart, which condition the outer world of human relationships and lead to decisions and actions. We are therefore involved in the science of psychology and the science of philosophy. We must understand and be able to answer that ancient ques-tion, *What is Man*? And we must understand and be able to practice the basic values—spiritual and mate-rial—on which the collective life we live on this small planet, Earth, can be rebuilt according to the clear requirements of a world which has already become *physically* one and interdependent.

Of the twenty-four books of Alice Bailey, all con-cerned with the unfoldment of consciousness and world reconstruction, five titles form a sequence of instruction, suggestion and guidelines for the future. These five volumes are published under the overall title of *A Treatise on the Seven Rays*. The first two are concerned with *Esoteric Psychology*; the third with *Esoteric Astrology*; the fourth with *Esoteric Healing*; and the fifth with *The Rays and the Initiations*. All five contain a wealth of information and teaching, which many would probably dismiss as unprovable nonsense; but which today are finding a worldwide response in receptive, and enquiring minds.

The two volumes on *Esoteric Psychology* detail the constitution of man as a threefold being—spirit, soul and form, or life, consciousness and appearance— patterned precisely on the constitution of the one God, or living Intelligence, or Energy, however we may choose to name Him, Who is also a trinity, as well as a reflection of the same underlying energy pattern prevailing throughout the solar system and the cosmos. According to the Christian bible, "man is made in the image of God," and this is literally true in a psychological as well as in a phenomenal sense. "As above, so below," is a well-known aphorism in esoteric teaching, with the reverse equally valid—as below, so above.

Working and thinking "from the universal to the particular," if we can begin to understand the energies, the relationships and the states of consciousness which condition that larger Life, of which we are all a part, then we can begin to see and to understand what an individual human being is, how he functions in response to the spark of indwelling divinity, as well as to external stimuli, and why the material rather than the spiritual aspect of life conditions human behaviour and relations for so long and often with such disastrous results.

Psychology today should be based on the fact of a human being as essentially threefold and spiritual in nature. He is spirit and soul, as well as body and form: he can become aware of that reality in him, and he can begin to transform his way of living—no matter how gross or how degenerate—by taking the first steps towards lifting his consciousness towards the inner spiritual self, the soul, or the Christ within. Psychology for long years has been based on the past or the lower aspects of human nature, on digging into and analysing the darkness of human errors and the baser instincts, instead of looking up and forward into the light, to the future, and working to establish a link, or alignment, with the one and only true source of transformation and redemption—the soul, the spiritual self.

A well-known Italian psychologist, Dr. Roberto Assagioli (who died a few years ago) has been one of the first to establish his professional work on this basis, and many have learned from him and with him, and are continuing his methods. He called his method *Psychosynthesis*, and established the Institute of Psychosynthesis, which has spread around the world today. This is a derivation of the material in Alice Bailey's books, a practical interpretation, put into daily, practical use in professional diagnosis and prescription. It sets the individual search for the real self, the spiritual man, the true "psyche," the soul, using visualisation, meditation, and the acquisition of knowledge which sharpens and develops the mind and which, when blended with the loving understanding of an awakening heart, can lead to wise living.

In this process the energies available to us for use are of superlative importance, for, to use another esoteric aphorism, "all is energy, and energy follows and conforms itself to thought." Hence the importance of a clear, open, unbiassed, well-stocked mind. All is energy; all is living substance, qualified by life and developing some form of consciousness. There is no such thing as "inorganic substance." All matter, all the substance which makes up the various kingdoms in nature—human, animal, vegetable and mineral—is endowed and imbued with the same living energy derived from the same divine source. The difference lies within the various states of consciousness in the different kingdoms, from the evolving, awakening consciousness of a man and woman to become a fully aware and functioning unit of spiritual life, to the relatively inert, crystallised and "unconscious" state of the substance of the mineral kingdom. But all is evolving, slowly but surely; and in the human kingdom we have the power to choose to cooperate with our own evolutionary process, to hasten our emergence from a material to a spiritual focus and way of life, to become a conscious contributor to the evolutionary process proceeding within our planet as a whole. We have that choice.

And the energies we need in our efforts are always available to us. Orthodox scientists have already determined that cosmic rays are constantly pouring throughout the solar system, bombarding all forms within it with invisible but powerful energies. Esoteric science perceives these energies as emanations from potent Beings, or Entities—energy centres— within the universe; and this is where esoteric astrology comes into our picture. Esoteric astrology has little to do with charts or horoscopes, except incidentally; esoteric astrology is called, in Alice Bailey's book of that name, the science of relationships, relationships between the energies embodied in the forms of planets, and stars and suns. In the light of our intense interest in space over recent years, and our intention to utilise space, Governor Jerry Brown had an interesting comment to make in his article in the New York Times: "Space, far from its popular image as a useless vacuum, is an ocean rich with energy, materials and opportunities." According to esoteric astrology "Space is an entity," a great, all-encompassing living Being, within Whose body of manifestation are found certain areas, or centres, of living energy, just as these centres exist also in a human being. And there are seven basic types of energy which produce, among other results, seven basic types of human being, depending upon the type of energy influencing the soul principle of each person. These seven ray types of energy are:

first ray—the energy of will or purpose
second ray—the energy of love and wisdom
third ray—the energy of active, or creative,
      intelligence
fourth ray—the energy of harmony through conflict
fifth ray—the energy of concrete knowledge, or
      science
sixth ray—the energy of devotion or abstract
      idealism
seventh ray—the energy of order, or ceremonial
      magic.

The first three, the rays of will or purpose, of love and wisdom, and of active intelligence, are the major energies at the present time; and all cycle in and out of manifestation over vast periods of time, so that some are more dominant and influential than others at any one time. At the end and the beginning of an age, which we experience today, it always seems that the precise energies we need to help us move forward into new experience with the capacity to change in response to the world of the future, are those that are most influential. And today, as we are moving forward into the incoming age of Aquarius, the dominant ray energies are these: the *first* ray—*will or purpose*, and if ever we needed a sense of purpose and the will to put it into effect, surely that time is now; the *second* ray—*love and wisdom*, which is the dominant ray energy of our solar system now and for a vast period of time to come; and how else but through love, and its wise use, can we ever establish those right human relationships and practical brotherhood which alone will enable us to survive into the future?; the *seventh* ray — *order and organisation*, and a sense of right relationship, of rhythm, beauty and the ritualistic use of time, which will help us to respond rightly to the white magic of the soul principle.

The *third* ray energy of *active and creative intelligence* is always available because our planetary Life is controlled by it during this world cycle; *fourth* ray energy is also always available because it is the dominant energy at present controlling humanity — this is the energy of *harmony through conflict* — and that really speaks for itself! In practically every case of significant human relationships, it seems we can only arrive at an eventual harmony through an interim long or short term period of conflict and confrontation.

And incidentally, according to Alice Bailey's books, each age or era in history is influenced by one or more types of energy as a dominant force, in the midst of whatever other energies may be available. With the entry at present into the age of Aquarius, *sixth* ray energy of *idealism and devotion* is being withdrawn and seventh ray energy is coming through into manifestation much more potently. It is sixth ray energy which has, during the 2000 or so years of the outgoing Piscean era, helped to develop a spiritual sensitivity and idealism in humanity which, in many cases today, tends towards a form of fanaticism and crystallisation. The incoming seventh ray energy, on the other hand, gives us what we need now to help us understand and include the peoples of other nations and cultures and to learn to live together in right relationship and at peace.

This is a brief and necessarily incomplete picture of the available energies, according to the seven rays involved, because these energies inter-relate in various ways, and from various sources, to influence human behaviour and response to opportunity. But, generally speaking, this shows something of what the esotericist understands by the energy of the rays and the influence it can have on human consciousness and human affairs.

Psychology, then, is—or should be—understood as the science of the soul, the true psyche, the conscious-ness aspect of man and God. Esoteric psychology shows how that essential relationship between man and God can be consciously "brought to life." It shows how an individual can become responsive to the soul, the Christ principle, the "God within"; how the lower personality characteristics can be transformed by the power of the indwelling soul as soul values are built into the daily life to replace those of more materialis-tic and selfish standards. In other words, esoteric psy-chology takes as literal fact that the psyche, or soul, is the concern of psychology, not in any abstract or theoretical way, but as an attainable, practical method of correcting and sublimating the errors, problems and sufferings of the personality by the loving, intelligent power of the soul. In this way, humanity as a whole, and world problems generally, can be led towards the changes necessary to produce the civilisation of the future, right human relationships and a world at peace.

In fact, esotericism itself is best defined as the sci-ence of the redeeming soul, the science of redemp-tion. There is nothing "secret" about esotericism as is so often thought. But it is concerned with the inner, subjective, and less visible aspects of human nature, with the meaning and quality of life, and with the subjective causes from which outer effects stem. The forms of life that are visible to our eyes, are but the tip of the iceberg when it comes to answering the question, "What is man?" And this is where esoteric philosophy enters into the whole structure of human development and evolution. Philosophy deals with the principles, the ideas and the laws which, if allowed, tend to influence human attitudes and actions and to develop ethical and moral standards. Esoteric philos-ophy, like esoteric psychology and the whole range of esotericism, is an extension of what has been called the "Ageless Wisdom" teaching. The Ageless Wisdom is a body of knowledge—and of wisdom derived from experimentation and experience with that knowledge—which has always been available to those who genuinely and selflessly seek for the answers to the basic problems of human life on this planet. The Wisdom teaching has been interpreted and re-interpreted throughout the ages according to current need and the condition of human consciousness. It underlies all the major world religions and all authentic modern esoteric teaching; it can be summarised for today's world in a few basic laws and principles:

The Law of Right Human Relations:	The Principle of Goodwill
The Law of Group Endeavour:	The Principle of Unanimity
The Law of Spiritual Approach:	The Principle of Essential Divinity

These, put into practice on the wings of the three major streams of energy—the dynamism of the "peaceful, silent will," the power of love, and the creativity of active intelligence—can revolutionise our ways of thinking, of living and acting, in our own affairs, and in relationship with our fellowmen.

Volumes IV and V in this series of books on the Seven Rays, also show how the ray energies act and interact with the forces present in life as we have created it. *Esoteric Healing* (Volume IV) gives the Laws and Rules for healing according to the spiritual requirements of this exact and exacting science. While all would-be healers are directed towards the acquisition of practical knowledge concerning the physical constitution of a human being, they are also required to become sensitive to the psychological factors and, in particular, to the intent of the soul. The requirements are, therefore, far from easy to fulfill; and the use of modern medical science is always recommended as an essential support to the structure of creating a condition of health throughout the whole, threefold constitution of a human being.

The fifth, and final, volume in this Treatise on the Seven Rays (*The Rays and the Initiations*) goes in detail into the Fourteen Rules for group work and group initiation. The nine planetary initiations are also discussed, in detail, as to their interrelationship both with human evolution and with the governing ray energies. It is a book of advanced teaching, invaluable to those who are consciously seeking to unfold their spiritual potential and resources, and to bring themselves into alignment with the inner, energy structure within the planetary Life. Individual spiritual development is not a major concern, however, although individual growth may be an original part of the motive inspiring search into esoteric teachings. Essentially, we find, in seeking to apply the Rules for Group Growth in the way we live, that attention changes from personal benefit and growth, to the need for cooperation with the spiritual growth possible to humanity as a whole; and consequently the whole orientation changes from personal "salvation" to "service," and from service to identification with the process of evolution proceeding in an orderly manner throughout the whole planet, from the lowest forms of unevolved life to the most divinely unfolded and inspired.

There are methods and techniques to be learned; but the work is done and the transformation made in consciousness by the way we are able to live what we know, to become what we essentially are as an incarnated fragment of divine life, and to contribute to an all-encompassing Purpose we may not know in detail, or understand, but which we can help to work out as we "let" the energies of light and love and the will-to-good control our lives, our motives and our relationships.

Initiation means a continuing movement forward into greater light, a constantly unfolding and expanding consciousness, and identification with one's soul group for service purposes, and—ultimately—that sense of universality which brings us into alignment with the energy channels throughout the planet through which humanity can be transfigured, negativity can be transmuted, and the whole of our way of life on Earth can be transformed.

Briefly, and therefore inadequately, this is what esotericism is all about and this is what Alice Bailey's books present in numerous ways and in different relationships.

CHAPTER 8—Leadership: Spiritual or Esoteric*

This matter of leadership—what it is and how it should be exercised—is emerging today in the forefront of human consciousness as a vital issue to be faced and understood. This is happening, I believe, because we seem to be so bereft of inspired and inspiring leadership, particularly in political and governmental areas of both national and international importance.

This growing concern isn't really surprising because of the increasingly evident power play among the nations of the world, large and small, as each one seeks to impose its own national self-interest on all the rest, rather than to seek out the underlying causes in international differences so as to come, *together*, to an agreed and genuine compromise in which all may benefit. Compromise, in the overall interest, demands leadership of vision and wisdom.

This sort of polarised struggle always seems to emerge in one form or another at the end of a major world period and the beginning of a new, such as we experience today. It seems to be more apparent today than at any time in history, no doubt because of our modern technology and means of instantaneous electronic communication. We can all, practically everywhere in the world, hear, see and know, what is happening everywhere else, and we can all develop our own opinions as intelligent contributions to an informed public opinion.

National and world events are paralleled in importance by the individuals, or groups, who cause and

---

* An address given at the Easter Festival of the Meditation Group for the New Age, Ojai, California, April 1985.

direct the happenings. In other words, by the leaders in world thought and world action. We see them in the context of their national, religious, racial or social background; or, we see the effects they have, for good or ill, not only in their own environment, but on a worldwide scale; for truly no nation "is an island complete unto itself."

Leadership is of many kinds, at many levels. Some deserve, or have earned, the right to exercise such a responsibility. Many have not, but acquire their power and authority by conscious and persistent effort, sometimes ruthlessly or even illegally pursued, and selfishly and irresponsibly exercised. To adapt a well-known saying to our theme: Some are born leaders; some acquire leadership; and some have leadership thrust upon them. I have a real compassion for this third, sink or swim, category, having experienced it myself.

To touch for a moment on the *levels* of leadership; these, I think, are two in the main. There is the "outer" level, which is concerned with organisation, management, planning, and activity; and an "inner" level, which is responsible for vision, quality, values, and the maintenance of whatever ethical, moral and spiritual standards may pertain to an organisation, or an organism. In a real leader, in its deepest and most ideal sense, the two levels combine, complementing and supporting each other.

But in the last analysis, leadership is an aggregate of diverse qualities and capacities, fused into an integrated whole, actively manifesting a quality of life, and an understanding of life, somewhat beyond the average, and frequently beyond the understanding of the majority, which consequently often produces friction, criticism, and condemnation.

Leadership at this inner, or spiritual, level depends upon many qualifications. Good character is basic, of course, but not enough in itself. There has to be an incorruptible integrity, and a knowledge and acceptance of life on Earth as a manifestation of a divine essence; a recognition that what we see and hear and touch around us is merely the outer expression of an inner livingness, an energy, and a purpose, which emanate from a great Being, or Life, Whom many call "God." This is the one supreme Entity in Whom we all "live and move and have our being," and Whose life and love permeate with energy every atom of substance within this planet with a definite plan and purpose.

Spiritual leadership, as a manifestation of an innate divine essence, is dependent on the extent to which an individual has succeeded in unfolding, and evolving, that inherent capacity for goodness, or Godness, which provides the necessary vision and strength, and capacity in everyday life to influence one's environment. Therefore, it does not depend on many of the factors which govern our outer activities and relationships, although spirituality must be intelligently and pragmatically interpreted and applied. And it supersedes such considerations as sex, race, religious forms, economic or social standards. Anyone, of either sex, of any race, religion, national or cultural background, can be born with the spiritual qualities of leadership well developed, or be placed at birth in circumstances where the opportunity to acquire the qualities of leadership, or to have leadership "thrust upon them," may be a natural next step in that person's evolving spiritual consciousness.

Of course, all this depends upon a basic factor—the doctrine of reincarnation. Reincarnation provides for the evolution of consciousness in form during life after life, in conformity with the purpose of God's manifestation within this planet Earth to develop and reveal the divinity inherent in every atom of substance, thus redeeming and transforming the way we all, men and women alike, govern our affairs and conduct our human relationships.

Through often painful experience we learn "by means of evil that good is best," as somebody has expressed it; or, sometimes we wilfully, or helplessly, delay the learning process of growth. But we all go through the purifying experiences of suffering, caused by ignorance, by our own mistakes, by fear, by separateness, or by inexplicable sorrows and deprivations. In the course of many lives there is nothing we do not touch and know and live through, sometimes over and over again, until the needed lessons are learned.

But eventually we do learn not to go on making the same wilful, or foolish, mistakes, and gradually a new awareness of the true values in life begins to emerge, and a demand for better personal standards of ethics and morals and spiritual values, as a guiding light through the vicissitudes of daily life, wherever one's path may lead.

But even this isn't enough. "Made in the image of God," and bearing the imprint of that divine signature within us, we are expected by those further along in evolution than we are, to "*reveal* divinity," not by what we say but by the way we live, no matter how clumsily we may interpret and express it. And so, eventually, by practice "to make perfect."

We are the custodians and the servers of a great Plan and Purpose. But while Martin Luther King, who was dazzled by a vision of the promised land seen from the mountain top, knew that he might not reach it, we also know that the work of redemption and revelation takes place in the valleys of human life, where the problems lie, and through the redemptive influence of living service in the place where we are.

Strengthening the Light in Others

The message of the Buddha—the "Supremely Enlightened One," as Buddhists call him—was, "Be ye a *lamp* unto your own feet." By committing ourselves in sacrifice and service to the Light, which we all must eventually reveal, we encourage, support, inspire and strengthen the light in others and for others. We stimulate leadership potential wherever it may exist, and in whatever context, and we assume responsibility—the personal responsibility—of "letting our light shine," that is, of living a life governed and controlled by spiritual values in whatever corner of the world we find ourselves.

It is out of all this growth and evolutionary development, over centuries of time, that real leadership emerges. True leadership—that is, the ability to inspire, enlighten and stimulate others—is the acme and the essence of many lives of loving service. As was said of the Christ, "the greatest among you is the servant of all." And this is so fundamental an aspect of leadership that it can offer guidelines of discrimination and evaluation when we are, personally, involved in the need to decide and conclude what *we* understand by leadership and what *we* are prepared to accept.

We are all familiar with at least some of the many definitions given to the word "spiritual" by the Tibetan Master, Djwhal Khul, in Alice Bailey's books. We know, therefore, that there is a distinction in meaning between what is "spiritual" and what is "religious." Many aspects of life and many human activities are spiritual in nature because they contribute to the improvement and progress of human living conditions and human understanding and relationships, although no *religious* forms or beliefs may be involved.

Widespread Spiritual Leadership

Spiritual leadership, in this sense, is therefore probably far more widespread than we realise. All those who serve in their own chosen fields and activities with integrity, with love for humanity, and upon a sound basis of ethical and moral values, are exercising a genuine and much needed form of spiritual leadership which encourages the relegation of form and materialistic values to their rightful place. We cannot live and learn and grow except through the right use of all the resources of this planet, and this includes matter and form. A "new materialism" is now in process of dawning on our consciousness as the new age of Aquarius unfolds. And it is the spiritual leadership of those who have brought the form side in their own lives into perspective and under control which today acts as the forward-moving, evolutionary cutting edge within human consciousness as a whole. This phenomenon is evident in science, in education, in all forms of social programmes and affairs, in business and commerce, in the home, and—yes—even today in embryonic form in the political and governmental worlds, the most difficult of all.

In all areas of human life we find members of the new group of world servers serving in their own way in their own place, many—or most—of them what we call the "unconscious" disciples of the Hierarchy and the Christ, unaware in their brain cells of the source and origin of their moral convictions or where those convictions will eventually lead them. These constitute the leaven in the human dough of mediocrity, the raising and lifting ingredient for millions upon millions of unknown contemporaries and for the unborn of the future.

And there is another element in all this, which is really our major interest: that minute aspect of the world consciousness and the world servers which we call esoteric. These conscious disciples of the planetary and the solar hierarchies know—or should know, and can and will know—something of the inner spiritual structure of the system in which we live. On these few—increasing in numbers as the years go by—rests the pioneering responsibility of self-control in all aspects of one's personal life, leading eventually to the degree of control, mastery, and planetary service characteristic of the spiritual Hierarchy itself.

Leadership, in this sense and in this area of life and consciousness by these conscious disciples and esoteric servers, requires a different understanding, a different level of self-forgetfulness and sacrificial will, and an involvement in planetary service which supersedes the narrow limits of any specialised activity common to the normal routine of human behaviour. The requirements and qualifications for world discipleship and for leadership in the esoteric field are exacting and unprecedented. This is where we might focus our thoughts now.

What is the major distinction between an *esoteric* group and a spiritual group? I would say that it is the *conscious* hierarchical link of an esoteric group or individual; plus the ability to *practise the principles* of ashramic work and esoteric teaching.

The esoteric servers and serving groups, in the world, as they exist today in more or less embryonic form for future expansion, are unique in history. They consist of those who have reached, and gone beyond, that state of spiritual growth which is the normal outcome of a steadily evolving consciousness. At a certain stage of growth, the *automatic* process of evolution can go no further because the limits of a purely human response to spiritual stimulation have been reached. To go further requires conscious choice, conscious effort, deliberate search, and the registered intention of the soul itself to use whatever resources may be available to take the would-be disciple forward to the next spiritual step into the unknown. This is the most dramatic and significant stage in the evolution of a potential esoteric server, accepting responsibility for his own evolution, and responding, as a soul, to the call of Hierarchy. And many hesitate and delay such a fateful step from which the personality, on its own, shrinks in apprehension, sensing the demands and the difficulties ahead and the "forcing process," as D.K. calls it. Such a forcing process is imposed by the soul and the Master of the ashram, as the goals and motives of the Hierarchy — the great ashram of Sanat Kumara — replace those of the individual personality.

The major difference, then, between the spiritually (if unconsciously) motivated men and women of good-will, and the growing group of esoteric servers, is the *conscious* choice to develop, to express, and to reveal the divinity inherent in the soul principle, the indwelling Christ, and, by such a fixed intention, to become directly associated with the fifth kingdom in nature, the spiritual Hierarchy of the planet, led by the Christ.

This growing group of esotericists in the world, disproportionately tiny as it is, forms the vital/etheric heart centre of the new group of world servers. It anchors the planetary lifeline in material substance; it conveys the energy flow of the planetary Logos throughout His whole body of manifestation in the form of sound vision, inspired ideas, loving and inclusive understanding, creative intelligence, and an irreversible and irresistibly potent will-to-good. And, most important of all from the standpoint of the Hierarchy, it is a living *demonstration* within the human — the fourth — kingdom that what D.K. calls "the great chain of Hierarchy" extends, lovingly, throughout the planetary body, providing not only the *structure* which maintains the physical framework, but also — like the spinal cord in an individual — the vital channels for the circulation of all the fluids the blood needs to maintain its healthy function. "The blood is the life," and the chain of Hierarchy is the lifeline within the planetary body of manifestation, in which the new group of world servers now occupies its central position.

So the esoteric group in the world has a far greater significance to the Hierarchy than its function as a pioneering group of world servers, meeting the critical needs of this climactic period of transition between the old age and the new.

D.K. has said that every real esotericist is, automatically, both a healer and a teacher. I would also add, a *leader*, not striding out ahead of everyone else — that isn't leadership — but by the force of a living example. This is a matter of radiation which, in turn, depends upon the actual state of being. The key word for every individual and every group striving to move towards the Hierarchy is, therefore, *grow*, no matter how or by what means, but *grow*.

A true esoteric group automatically and without any fixed intention provides a form of subjective leadership to which all in the group contribute. Yet that leadership quality must, of necessity, permeate through into daily life and day-to-day conditions and relationships. And it is here, within the many groups and among the many esoteric servers that clarity of thought is needed, because confusion does exist. This confusion is compounded also by the recognised and accepted fact that with the changing energy flow and changing objectives of the Aquarian age, our understanding of what leadership means in an esoteric group must also change. Too many tend to see such a change as the obvious and necessary one from the more or less authoritarian, single leader at the centre of most Piscean age groups, building the group around him according to his own ideas and exercising a firm control, to the more Aquarian type of leadership by and as a group. But we don't yet know what group leadership in the Aquarian age really means, although we think we do when we give the term the most obvious and most superficial interpretation of our own literal, and limited, minds. Lack of clear and independent thought based on the principles of the teaching, seems to be the eternal human frailty. We throw out the baby with the bathwater and adapt the available teachings — which we most diligently search and excerpt — to our own fallible interpretations, selecting those that seem to support our own ideas and ignoring the rest.

We have been warned by D.K. not to make a Bible of his books, but we do it all the time. Taking selected extracts, which say what we want to hear, out of the immediate context in which they appear, and out of the context of the teaching as a whole, is usually a self-serving exercise, revealing little of the realities on which esoteric teaching is based, and contributing nothing to growth in our own understanding or to group understanding of the real needs and the real meaning of what we read.

Yet the realities of esoteric leadership are, in fact, abundantly clear. I mentioned just now the "chain of Hierarchy." You will know D.K.'s statement that "there is naught but Hierarchy," the greatest, or highest, link being connected to the least or the lowest by all the evolving units of life which exist and grow along the whole evolutionary chain, each unit holding within it the same potential, the same pattern of energy flow, the same constitution as the solar Logos of our system, and the same constitution as Sanat Kumara Himself, our planetary Logos. It is only the degree of unfoldment of the potential which causes the distinctions and the differences.

A true esoteric group is linked, *consciously*, with the spiritual Hierarchy, the great ashram of Sanat Kumara. The structure of a true esoteric group is, therefore, identical to that of the ashram; it is a "miniature Hierarchy" in itself, evolving, functioning and serving in the world of humanity on the well-known "as above, so below" principle.

So what is the ashramic pattern which esoteric groups should duplicate? Some rather fanatical, or narrow-eyed, seekers for the Aquarian group pattern reject altogether the idea of a "group leader", claiming that the group itself provides the needed incentive, vision and leadership. A passage taken out of context from Volume II of D.K.'s *Esoteric Psychology* (which also appears in your paper on Energising Thoughts) is often quoted to substantiate this misconception. "Leadership by a group" is certainly a new age ideal and one that is already emerging among the esoteric groups in the world. But this ideal does not in the least change the basic energy pattern of the group any more than it changes the hierarchical pattern of the ashram. The change needed is one of transformation of the group itself, from a *group of disciples* (a discipleship group) to the Aquarian meaning of a *group disciple*. There is a big and significant difference. A discipleship group consists of disciples of all stages of unfoldment, all rather more than less *individually* focussed and all sincerely seeking to put into practice the basic esoteric principles of group unity and group harmony. A group disciple, on the other hand, has achieved a more advanced and hierarchically integrated position, because group members have been able, in the interests of group work, to subjugate their individualities to the *group* soul, and to accept, with understanding and with joyous acquiescence, the ashramic pattern which must demonstrate in all group extensions of the spiritual Hierarchy.

That pattern is simple. It is based on the one, the three, the seven or the twelve—depending on the context—and the group membership as a whole through whom the energies flow out into organised activity.

D.K. always refers to the Christ as the "head" of the Hierarchy, and to the Hierarchy "led by the Christ." The Christ also functions as a triangle with two others at the head of the three major hierarchical departments, his own major responsibility being that great second ray energy department of religion and education, which occupies a major position in this second solar system under the influence of the second ray of love and wisdom.

Within each of the seven major ashrams the same basic pattern exists, which is also emerging in the seven subdivisions of each ashram. The hierarchical pattern is part of the planetary constitution for this cycle. We have no choice but to accept it. But, it is a pattern of *responsibility*, not of authority. The differences in spiritual unfoldment, which exist in the Hierarchy just as they do in outer esoteric groups, obviously mean that the ability to accept and discharge responsibility for planetary work varies greatly. And this seems to be necessary to the smooth functioning of an ashram, or of an ashramic group, because, as D.K. puts it, "it permits of a wide range of relationships." The ashram nevertheless functions as a *unity*, with complete integration and interrelationship with other ashrams. There is no sense of difference, or of superiority or inferiority, because these do not exist. There is a recognition of spiritual "place," both one's own and that of other group members, and a complete acceptance and sense of identity with those more advanced and those less advanced than oneself.

Such a group uses the science of group impression to receive the ideas, the vision and the inspiration pertinent to the next step ahead for humanity. This is not necessarily received in an identical or simultaneous form by all in the group, but is recognised and supported by group acclaim or consensus, so that the work can proceed smoothly and without delay. Such a group, and there are few to be found, *is* a group leader so far as human consciousness and human affairs are concerned, although its inner structure is hierarchical in terms of energy, responsibility, and focal points of energy.

There are two (at least) points of real difficulty for many in making this transition to a group disciple patterned on the ashram. One is the sticking point of *authority*; and the other the equally difficult of individuality *vis-à-vis* group identification.

Functioning with Authority

With the realisation that the new age esoteric group will demonstrate such a unity of purpose that the group itself will fulfil a leadership role in human affairs, some of us are tending to confuse "authority" with "authoritarianism." Every member in such a group should function with a definite authority—the authority of love, the authority of soul contact, and the authority of the Hierarchy itself. But where any individual—or group—acts as an authoritarian or a totalitarian, imposing the will of one on others, there is obvious need for change. It has been my experience, however, that those who most loudly denounce or reject what they see as authority in others, are always those who, given the opportunity, are most likely to become authoritarian themselves. We do, after all, "look at others through the front half of our own aura"—one of Foster's favourite sayings.

But there must be a genuine spiritual authority within and behind the work of an esoteric group or world server, an authority based on personal experience which reveals the extent to which the individual or the group has become a conscious, integral part of that great centre of energy in which the Christ stands at the point of energy reception and distribution, representing the manifested principle of the Godhead. This is an authority which marks the clear empirical distinction between direct experience of truth and reality, and an intellectual acceptance of it; between the one whose focus of attention is upon himself as a would-be server and one whose attention rests wholly within the work itself. No one and no group functions in a leadership position without that direct experience which confers accuracy and confidence, and evokes recognition and response in others.

And what of that priceless possession, our own individual identity, our *self*-consciousness, which we struggle for so many lifetimes to perfect?

End of Separate Individuality

The on-going process of growth brings us finally to the point where we must be *willing* to accept the fact that, like the soul itself, our separate individuality also drops away, discarded as an outgrown tool, useful and necessary in its time, but no more than a hindrance to be overcome where the functioning of a group disciple is concerned.

The Fourteen Rules for Group Initiation published in Volume V of *A Treatise on the Seven Rays* series goes extensively into this process of shedding the outgrown aspects of the individual discipleship self. If we have the eyes to see and the ears to hear, we can learn much. The process is one of individualisation/ initiation/identification. A group disciple today is placed at the transition stage between initiation and identification. D.K. tells us that we probably cannot really understand what identification means, and of course he is right if we think that such a state of consciousness can be mentally perceived or even intuitively understood. It can only be known through experience and by the gradual transference of a separate individuality into a condition of identity with larger and larger wholes. It is simply the giving up of a lesser and more limited stage for something larger, more inclusive and of greater usefulness.

We are given much instruction and many hints to ponder in the Fourteen Rules, none of the real meaning apparent on the surface. A basic clue to the experience of identification which we all must someday experience—is given in Rule VIII. We are told that, under the Law of the Supplementary Seven, the group must "understand the Three and then the One. This they can do with the united breath and the unified rhythm." The united breath and the unified rhythm; these words we must each interpret for ourselves, they hold the key to the mystery of identification and also to the process of transition from a discipleship group to a group disciple.

The outstanding characteristic of a group disciple, therefore, is not so much *synthesis*, for this is an obvious and essential requirement, but identification, progressive identification with the larger wholes of which we are a part—the esoteric group disciple in which we serve, the new group of world servers in which the fire of our fierce determination to be ourselves dies out, the planetary whole in which we realise our identification as an integral part of the great and complex structure of our God, and the universal whole of the solar system, which forms the field of service as well as the place of identification of Sanat Kumara.

No one can interpret words or the meaning of identification for another. It is those who do so who penetrate, esoterically, by living the teaching, who do begin to achieve some measure of identification with the whole of life and freedom from the limitations of their own individuality, and who serve to pioneer the way, to lead humanity forward into the new yoga of the Aquarian age, the yoga of synthesis.

So let's wrap all this up, if we can, within the main theme of this conference; leadership in its spiritual and essential form.

The paper of preparatory thoughts which contains the quotation from *Esoteric Psychology* about group leadership, opens with an excerpt from the book *Hierarchy*: "What state flourishes without a great Leader? What affirmed beginning has existed without a Leader? Verily one must understand that the concept of Leader is the synthesis of the highest strivings. Thus, only the concept of Hierarchy, or an Illumined Leader, can direct the spirit. Thus let all, all, ponder upon and remember the might of Hierarchy. Only through this understanding can one attain."

Both excerpts are definite and precise. They appear to be saying two different things; yet, they are not contradictory. They are saying the same thing in effect: that is, that while group disciples—and groups of disciples in their own place within the chain of Hierarchy—must and will in the future assume leadership roles within the evolution of consciousness and the reconstruction of the world, the interior spiritual structure of such groups duplicates, inevitably, the structure of the ashram. The pattern of the Hierarchy is repeated at the human level, a pattern which is based upon profound cosmic principles and well-established rhythms of energy flow and energy relationships.

Can you imagine the Hierarchy without its focal point, the Christ? Can you imagine an ashram without the Master? "At the centre of every esoteric group," A.A.B. once said, "stands a world disciple." The responsibility of that focal point—the world disciple, the Master of an ashram and the Christ at the heart of Hierarchy—is to receive and transmit energy and vision, to coordinate, integrate and synthesise, to generate cohesive and intelligent activity, and to make sure that there is an unimpeded communication and interrelationship throughout the whole group, from the centre to the periphery and from the periphery to the centre, including all wherever they may stand in unfoldment and accepted responsibility, consequently assuring that the outward flow into humanity itself will reach out with what is needed, when and where needed.

We know from the teaching that the "perfect group" includes individuals at different levels of spiritual unfoldment, facing different initiations, and functioning on all the seven rays of energy, even though the group as a whole is undergoing the process of some one initiation. This makes for internal difficulties at times, if individuals are not selfless enough or mature enough to accept others, with all their distinctions, as equally valuable and needed contributors to group good and to the group work. The group soul, in which all participate, is an abstract idea to many and a difficult one to materialise in living form.

Because the Master cannot function without the ashram, and the Christ cannot function without the Hierarchy, the focal point at the centre of an esoteric group cannot function without the group. The group itself as an entity, an organism, is responsible for registering the work of the future and for deciding how and when to do what, no matter whose words may first introduce a thought or a possibility. The group itself accepts a leadership role by the mere fact of its existence as a link in the hierarchical chain, a leadership not of power and authority, but in terms of responsibility, vision, and loving, creative activity. The old ideas certainly need change as new vision comes in, but the realities need to be preserved because, on the pattern of the ashram and using the hierarchical method, the evolution of our human institutions rests. Democracy is not the ultimate pattern of the future, D.K. tells us, any more than totalitarianism is a correct method to use today.

The embryonic foundations of the future hierarchical pattern already exist, as D.K. points out, in the national leader of a state, whether it be a President, a Prime Minister, or Chairman of a party, and two who make up the central triangle of national responsibility — one concerned with home or internal affairs, and the other with foreign or external policies. The *idea* is established because it's practical and sensible and it works. Even if we tried, causing disruption and division by our efforts, we could not change that deep-seated, profoundly subjective method of energy communication.

I have sometimes thought that, even mathematically, using the correct instruments, one cannot create a true circle without first establishing a centre. God is, after all, the Great Geometrician.

As always, we each come to our own points of growth and change and new revelation, and we each must interpret the teaching and make it real for ourselves. So that, eventually, with the love and support of all who work with us, now today as our peers, those to whom we look for inspiration, and those whom we in turn can inspire, we can truly and selflessly serve as a conscious and usable link within the great chain of Hierarchy. And this is the role for which the Hierarchy is preparing us.

CHAPTER 9—The Impact of the Wesak Festival*

There is always an inner quietness and peace surrounding the Wesak Festival which I suppose is the
result of the Shamballa influence, the peaceful, silent
Will, and I hesitate to break into it—but we must!

This is the spiritual highpoint of the year, the Wesak
Festival, and we know that the keynote and the observance of the Wesak Festival are in process of change.
They are going through a transition period, and have
not yet emerged into what may well become the new
keynote and the new age methods of observing this
high point of the year.

I expect we are all reasonably familiar with the
story of the legend of the actual Festival itself as it is
held in the Vaisaka valley in the Himalayas. This is a
time when the Christ and the members of the Hierarchy, the ranked initiates and disciples, and those who
are able to be present in either physical form or in
etheric form, gather together in the valley facing an
enormous, altar like rock on which stands a crystal
bowl of water. And we're told that there is a weaving
and a chanting and different symbols are formed by
the people who gather there. At the moment of the
full moon, or shortly before, an intense silence settles
down over the valley, and at the actual moment of
the full moon the Buddha can be seen, bathed in light
and colour, making his descent from the centre Shamballa, the centre where the Will of God is known, to
bring to humanity by way of those assembled in the
valley the blessing of the Father. The energy of that

---

* Address given at the Wesak Festival, May 1984, New York.

blessing impregnates the receptive bowl of water, and as the Buddha disappears the magnetised water is shared among those who are present and who directly participate in the ceremony.

I see no reason to doubt that that ceremony is still held each year, because obviously its physical location would be well protected and would be quite safe from detection and interference. And tonight, since we are in a transition period where the Wesak Festival and the basic, major keynote of the Festival are concerned, I want us to stick as closely as possible to what we know of the real meaning, the fundamentals, of the Wesak Festival and the teaching of the Lord Buddha. The legacy of the Buddha was responsible for the work that the Christ was able to do, and its influence is still pervasive and profound throughout the consciousness of the human race. It is still relevant and still as necessary today as it was when the Buddha first gave it 2500 years ago.

First of all, I think we might look briefly at something of the hierarchical background of the Wesak Festival ceremony. We're given to understand that it's only from the beginning of this century, from the year 1900, that humanity, members of the human kingdom, have been able to provide any form of acceptable and useful cooperation with the Wesak Festival. And we're also told that the effort has been made since 1900 by the Hierarchy to bring to the attention of the public the fact of the two Avatars, the Buddha and the Christ, both of them functioning on the second ray of Love-Wisdom. These Avatars were the first of our humanity to appear as human-divine Avatars, and to embody certain cosmic principles and to give them form. The Buddha embodied the principle of light, and because of that embodiment the Christ was able to embody the principle of love, and members of the human kingdom have recognised and affirmed that embodied Christ principle.

But the task of the Buddha is nearly over. His task of keeping the channel open for the light to irradiate men's minds by piercing annually through light substance to the earth, is nearly completed. The time is imminent, according to the teaching, that "in the light, we shall see Light," in our own right.

We also know that every century there is what is called a special "centennial effort" by the Hierarchy. They make a concerted endeavour to bring to humanity the types of energies and the specific goals that are needed for the immediate period ahead. And we're given to understand that from the year 1966 to the end of this century that centennial effort is on a wider scale and involves more members of the spiritual Hierarchy than ever before. This century this effort includes the Christ himself for the first time.

"When the Christ comes at the close of this century and makes his power felt, he will come as the teacher of love and unity and the keynote he will strike will be regeneration, through love, poured forth on all humanity. This will demonstrate on the physical plane in the formation of active groups in every city of any size and in every country, which will work aggressively for unity, cooperation and brotherhood in every department of life: economic, religious, social and scientific. It is this impending probability which is held in mind for the remainder of this century at the annual recurrence of the Wesak Festival. As humanity sets up a current of thought by a similar concentration, an irresistible and evocative force is generated."

There is the hierarchical background and an indication of the forward looking impetus that is emerging from the Hierarchy and the Christ, and something of what the Wesak Festival should be able to accomplish in the years ahead through the instrumentality and the cooperation of increasing numbers of human beings.

So let's look at the energies that are available through the sign Taurus in which the Wesak Festival occurs, very briefly. First of all, the full moon which marks the actual moment of the Wesak Festival itself, the climax, will occur at 12:29 a.m. tomorrow morning. The keynote for Taurus, that well-known keynote: "I see, and when the eye is opened, all is Light." And the light of Taurus is the penetrating light of the Path of Return, the way that we all must tread, back to our origins, back to our spiritual source.

We're told that Taurus is the sign of the major life incentive, because the driving force behind all aspects of the unfolding Taurian consciousness is the Will of God. Will, power, desire, aspiration, ambition, motive, purpose, impulse, incentive, Plan; all these express one of the major underlying attributes and fundamental causes of manifestation and of the will-to-be or the will-to-live. And the triplicity of desire/aspiration/direction are words which describe the progress and the basis of: man the personality (desire), man the soul (aspiration), and man the channel for spirit or life (direction or will). All three point to the cause which underlies all events, all progress and all happenings in time and space.

It was the Buddha who clarified for us the nature of desire and its unfortunate results when unenlightened and undisciplined. The Christ emphasised the transmutation of desire into aspiration, an aspiration which has been largely a trusting conformity without real understanding of the Will of God. But with the opening of the Aquarian age and the direct impact of the Shamballa force during this century, and as it continues on throughout the coming century, there will no longer be a blind acquiescence in God's will, but an understanding cooperation with the divine Plan and an enlightened fusion of the individual will with the divine Will for the greater good of the whole subordinated to the divine urge for beauty, synthesis, and the free expression of the hidden divinity, the mystery at the heart of all form. And this indicates a response to the Shamballa experience, giving ever greater meaning to the Wesak Festival experience.

The Christ and the Buddha work together in the closest possible cooperation to bring about the maximum benefits and effects within the consciousness of the human race. And the energies and the specific qualities that each embody are both essential to this Festival purpose; the two must cooperate and work together. D.K. makes this remark: "Should the needed work be carried forward when the Wesak Festival comes around each year, then the necessary adjustments in the world can be made. The hoped for stimulation lies largely in the hands of a cooperating humanity." *It's our responsibility*. "If this work should prove a success, it should be possible to inaugurate a new relation between the Hierarchy and mankind. It should mark the beginning of a new type of mediatory work, work carried forward by a salvaging group of servers who are in training now for that group which will eventually save the world, the new group of world servers."

And of course there are special forces available at each of the three Festivals to augment the other types of energy that are being precipitated and poured into the planets. At this Festival, the Forces of Enlightenment are active. The Forces of Enlightenment lead humanity "from darkness to light." When let loose on Earth they produce a clear grasp of the Plan which the Hierarchy desires to work out, a revelation of the issues involved in their right and possible sequence. And they also give a sense of proportion to human thinking, plus an appreciation of the spiritual values which should determine objective policies. And isn't this so badly needed today and in this year of choice and decision when we need to deepen our sense of values? Here we have at this Wesak Festival, through the instrumentality of the Forces of Enlightenment, an opportunity to irradiate the consciousness of humanity as a whole with a new sense of spiritual values as a basis for objective work and decisions.

We're told that these Forces "salvage the cultural gains of the past and implement that new and better culture which will be distinctive of the new age." In other words, nothing of any spiritual value is ever discarded. The real values, to whatever extent they have been incorporated and made manifest in human affairs, are used as a foundation, a new starting point, as a spring-board from which we can move on to incorporate the new incoming qualities and experiences of the Aquarian era.

So let's touch briefly on some of the fundamental facts of the Wesak Festival itself and what it really means. I'm having to take this right out of the Tibetan's books. He says this:

> "The Wesak Festival has been held down the centuries in the well-known valley in the Himalayas in order: one, to substantiate the fact of Christ's physical presence among us ever since his so-called departure. Two, to prove on the physical plane the factual solidarity of the eastern and western approaches to God. Both the Christ and the Buddha are present. Three, to form a rallying point and a meeting place for those who annually, in synthesis and symbolically, link up and represent the Father's House, the Kingdom of God, and humanity. And four, to demonstrate the nature of the work of Christ as the great and chosen Intermediary, standing as the representative of the spiritual Hierarchy and as the leader of the new group of world servers, and in his person, voicing their demand for the factual recognition of the existence of the Kingdom of God on Earth here and now."

So the Wesak Festival stands for three clear and definite ideas: first, the Festival links the past with the present in a continuity of revelation and living truth. It links the East with the West, uniting the Christian tradition, the Buddhist and Hindu faiths and the aspiration of all believers, orthodox and unorthodox. And second, the Festival marks the highest point of spiritual achievement and alignment, releasing an unusual flow of life and spiritual stimulation, that is, of light and love. And third, through the united efforts of the Buddha and the Christ working in the closest cooperation, a channel of communication is opened between humanity and God through which the love and wisdom of God may flow into a needy world. A door is opened, making this two-way approach possible. And it is a two-way approach, because we can approach much more closely to the highest centre of divinity on the planet at this time, just as the Father's House, Shamballa, can make a direct and unimpeded approach to the human kingdom. This increased impact of spiritual force permits great expansions of consciousness and many disciples move forward upon the Path of Initiation and all of us are affected according to our own evolutionary status.

And then, in capsule form, what should be accomplished at each Wesak Festival? First, the releasing of certain energies, potently affecting humanity and stimulating the spirit of love, of brotherhood and of goodwill. Second, the fusion of men and women of goodwill in the world into an integrated, responsive whole. Just imagine that for a moment. At this Wesak Festival through the release of these tremendously potent and dynamic streams of energies, the men and women of goodwill in the world become fused into one integrated and responsive whole. Can we register that in consciousness? Can we imagine it, can we visualise it? Can we accept its truth and reality and cooperate with it? And then the third thing to be accomplished, is the invocation and response of certain great Beings who guide the planetary Hierarchy and stand behind our planetary evolution. These Beings respond to a sufficiently strong call from aspirants and disciples. And, fourth, the evocation of a potent and one-pointed activity by the Hierarchy of

Masters, those Illumined Minds, those Lords of Compassion, responsible for world direction. A responsive alignment can be achieved between the spiritual Hierarchy, under the direction of the Christ, the new group of world servers, men and women of all races, nations and religions, responsible for establishing right human relationships, and the masses of men and women who respond to the ideas and objectives of international understanding, economic interdependence and unity. And as these three groups are aligned, the gates of the new life can open and the inflow of new spiritual force take place. Such is the group objective.

And these are *possibilities*, these objectives can be accomplished. You know, that really is incredible. I think we need to study and think about these words and realise how much can be accomplished through the integration of the planetary centres, including the centre humanity, and through the evocative release of these tremendously potent and dynamic forces through the instrumentality of the Christ and the Buddha at this time every year, the high spiritual point of the year. It is possible at such a time for spiritual accomplishments which are unbelievable. It's difficult to imagine. We can dream about it, we can think about it, we can know that one day these things can be brought about through growth in human consciousness, through better understanding, through a more active and real cooperation of the peoples of the world, with a greater capacity in the serving disciples of the world to lose themselves in the Plan of Hierarchy and offer themselves for use to the Christ and to the Masters of the Wisdom. But these things can be accomplished *now*, not all at once, not perhaps with obvious and dramatic manifested results, but gradually, bit by bit, this infiltration is taking place, this pervasive spiritual effect is brought about, and the values by which humanity as a whole lives are being transformed and the choices we make are influenced. These things are possible now.

The whole emphasis of the Wesak Festival is on the possibility of a totally new response to light resulting in mental illumination, enlightened thinking. The year 1946 marked the establishing of a new ashram within the Hierarchy, a *Wisdom* ashram, an ashram focussing the quality and the energy of wisdom, the second aspect of the second ray of love-wisdom. And that ashram is under the control of the Buddha specifically, and of the Christ, and also of the third ray Master, the Master R., because of the necessity for intelligent, knowing, understanding, and the right application of light and love to world events, to human affairs. And I think we need to bear in mind, that so recently—the year after the ending of world war—it was possible for Hierarchy to establish this new Wisdom ashram. One wonders whether humanity had in fact, as a result of the war, acquired a little more understanding which provided the final impetus and permitted the Hierarchy to establish this new centre of lighted intelligence and understanding love within its periphery.

Light and love and spiritual healing can be released in a flood of power at this Festival and definite changes can be produced in human consciousness. So this is what we seek to do as we align ourselves with the Christ representing the Hierarchy, with the Lord Buddha representing Shamballa, the centre where the will of God is known, with the Forces of Enlightenment emanating from the heart of God, with the Spirit of Peace as that great Being overshadows the Christ, the Prince of Peace, and with the Avatar of Synthesis, who today stands with the Christ at the opening of the Aquarian era.

We're told that the new group of world servers as a whole works under the influence of Taurus, with its capacity to illumine, enlighten and inspire. And humanity, the world disciple, is also responding to this Taurian light. So there's hope for us! We *are* responsive to spiritual light and enlightenment. And we're asked this vital question: "Will this Taurian influence, reinforced by the incoming Shamballa force, produce the floodlight of inspiration of which Taurus is the custodian, or will it simply foment desire, increase selfishness and bring humanity to the fiery heights of self-interest instead of to the mountain of vision and initiation?" Which shall it be for humanity's future?

The teaching of the Lord Buddha over 2000 years ago contains the clue to the right answer to that question and to the right orientation of human behaviour in the creation of a unified global community. And I want now to focus our thought and attention for a little while on some of the actual words and teachings of the Buddha. This teaching is a thing of beauty in its utter simplicity. Listening to the words let us use the creative imagination to visualise the effects of putting these teachings into practice. All of these excerpts, I might add, are taken from Helena Roerich's book, *The Foundations of Buddhism*, which, in my opinion, is one of the finest of its kind.

So we come to the Lord Buddha. There does not exist a more beautiful appeal to the world (or a more appropriate one in 1984) than this constantly repeated affirmation of the Lord Buddha:

> "Brother, I do not come to offer you any dogmas and I do not ask you to believe in that which so many others believe. I only exhort you to independent enlightenment, to use your own mind, developing it instead of letting it become dull. I adjure you not to resemble beasts of prey or stupid sheep. I implore you to be men with right views, men who toil untiringly for the acquisition of real knowledge which will prevail over suffering."

And here are the words of the very brief first sermon of the Buddha to his disciples, his Bhikshus.

> "There are two extremes," said the Buddha, "which the man who has devoted himself to the

higher life ought not to follow. The habitual practice on the one hand of those things whereof the
attraction depends upon the passions, especially of
sensuality, a low and pagan way of seeking gratifi-
cation, unworthy, unprofitable and fit only for the
worldly-minded. And the habitual practice on the
other hand of self-mortification, which is not only
painful but is as unworthy and unprofitable as the
other. But the Tathagata has discovered . . . (the
Tathagata, the Buddha, I love the definition of
that, "the Supremely Enlightened One" . . .) the
Tathagata has discovered a middle path which
avoids these two extremities, a path which opens
the eyes and bestows understanding, which leads
to peace of mind, to the higher wisdom, to full
enlightenment. In a word, to Nirvana. And this is
the noble eight-fold path of right views, high aims,
kindly speech, upright conduct, a harmless livelihood, perseverance in well doing, intellectual activity and profound meditation.

Nay more, O Bhikshus, the first truth, the truth
about sorrow is this, birth is attended with pain
and so are decay and disease. and death. Union
with the unpleasant is painful and separation from
the pleasant, and any craving that is unsatisfied is
a condition of sorrow. Now all this amounts in short
to this: that wherever there are the conditions of
individuality, there are the conditions of sorrow. The
cause of sorrow is the thirst or craving that causes
the renewal of individual existence, is accompanied
by evil and is ever seeking satisfaction, now here,
now there. That is to say, the craving either for
sensual gratifications or for continued existence or
for the cessation of existence, this is the noble truth
concerning the origin of sorrow. Deliverance from
sorrow is the complete destruction, the laying aside,
the getting rid of, the being free from, the harbouring no longer of this passionate craving. This is the
noble truth concerning the destruction of sorrow.

The path which leads to the destruction of sorrow is this noble eight-fold path alone, namely, right views, high aims, kindly speech, upright conduct, a harmless livelihood, perseverance in well doing, intellectual activity and profound meditation. This is the noble truth of the path which leads to the destruction of sorrow."

He says, "Whoso is free from all sensual passions, is of pure heart, and has overcome selfishness, he alone is a true disciple of the Enlightened. Let him therefore cultivate inner perfection, the attainment of knowledge, equanimity and benevolence. Toward all living beings on earth and in the worlds beyond, the weak and the strong, the high and the low, the good and the bad, the near and the far, let him be well disposed. Let him deceive none, threaten none, hurt none. As a mother on her only child, so let him, full of compassion and benevolence, look upon all beings every day and every hour. As a deep mountain lake, pure and unruffled be the spirit of him who walks along the Noble Eight-fold Path."

And the Buddha stresses the eternal verities of truth and beauty and goodness and the energies needed to manifest the verities, light and love and the will-to-good. Joy, love, compassion, patience are virtues always emphasised by Buddha. Energy and will arm the pupil with patience. "Energy and will produce patience and sustained control. Patience is born of compassion and, knowledge."

Buddha valued especially the evidence of effort. He never taught the *subjugation* of passions, but the transmutation and sublimation of their quality, for at the base of each passion is contained the spark of energy without which no progress is possible.

His Laws were the Law of Fearlessness, the Law of the renunciation of property, the Law of the evaluation of labour, the Law of the dignity of human personality, beyond caste and all outer distinction, the

Law of true knowledge, the Law of love based on self-knowledge.

Nothing exists without cooperation, he taught. In the whole universe only correlatives exist. "The selfish and conceited one could not build the future because, by cosmic Law, he would be outside the current of life which carries all that exists towards perfection." I think that should be a source of encouragement to us when we sometimes despair over the apparent success of the unworthy. The unworthy cannot build the future because it is "outside the current of life." It can create and establish an illusion only which is temporary and ephemeral and that is all.

Buddha found the way to the hearts of people, not through miracles, but by practical teaching of the perfection of everyday life and by his personal example of great cooperation. He never spoke against the rituals and beliefs of others. "Reverence your belief and never condemn the belief of others." He was concerned only with a broad and general understanding.

The teaching is salvation, not because it was given by Buddha but because it liberates. Life should be free and joyous. These are the great treasures in life and love is the greatest blessing of all because "love is mind-delivering." Love liberates the mind from its prison of insularity and bias. The greatest of all is the loving heart. And Buddha's love was of so immeasurable a stream that it could not be exhausted by any hate or hostility. On the contrary, a hostile attack only brought it to fuller unfoldment. Therefore he decreed that his disciples should act thus:

"However men may speak concerning you, whether appropriately or inappropriately, whether courteously or rudely, whether wisely or foolishly, whether kindly or maliciously, thus my disciples must you train yourselves. Our minds should remain unsullied. Neither should evil words escape our lips. Kind and compassionate will we ever remain, loving of heart, not harbouring secret hate. And we will bathe them with the unfailing stream of loving thought. And proceeding further, we will embrace and flood the whole wide world with constant thoughts of loving kindness, wide, ample, expanding, immeasurable as the world, free from enmity, free from ill will. Thus disciples must you train yourselves."

I wish I could go on with the remainder of those I have here, but there are too many. We should, however, recall the Buddha's reference to the Christ: "The time of the 'era of Maitreya' is at hand. All the Buddhas of the past have combined their wisdom of experience and handed it on to the Blessed Coming One."

And let us think about these words from the *Reappearance of the Christ*:

"The work of the Buddha for humanity is nearly over and his long alliance with the human race has nearly come to an end. The moment that the appearance of the Christ is an accomplished fact and the rule of right human relations is beginning definitely to condition human living, then the Buddha will pass to the work which awaits him. The intelligence principle of knowledge, which is the outstanding characteristic of humanity, will by then have been to a large extent transmuted into wisdom by the world intelligentsia. Wisdom is the predominant characteristic of the Buddha and the momentum of this wisdom energy will eventually be so strong that it will need no further distribution or control by him. He can then reorient himself to higher spheres of activity where his true work lies, and begin to work with an aspect of wisdom of which we know nothing. Later, through the cooperation of the Avatar of Synthesis, Christ will be able to blend within himself both of these major divine energies and thus be a pure expression of love and wisdom, of right relationship and of intuitive understanding."

And here is a symbol I would like us to hold in mind as we go into our meditation and as we approach the peak of the Wesak Festival experience and go on about our normal daily life. Here is a vitally significant symbol. It's the symbol of the Triangle of Energies standing behind the Christ, the symbol that includes the Avatar of Synthesis, that great Being Who, as it is said, "keeps His eye upon him, His hand beneath him, and His Heart in unison with his." And the second point is that Spirit of Peace, Who today is overshadowing the Christ, the Prince of Peace. And the third point of the triangle is the Lord Buddha, who "stands beside his brother in humble recognition of his great task." From the centre of this triangle the Christ works.

"When the Christ, the Avatar of Love, makes his reappearance then will the *Sons of men who are now the Sons of God* withdraw their faces from the shining light and radiate that light upon the *sons of men who know not yet they are the Sons of God*. Then shall the Coming One appear, His footsteps hastened through the valley of the shadow by the One of awful power Who stands upon the mountain top, breathing out love eternal, light supernal and peaceful, silent Will.

Then will the sons of men respond. Then will a newer light shine forth into the dismal, weary vale of earth. Then will new life course through the veins of men, and then will their vision compass all the ways of what may be.

So peace will come again on earth, but a peace unlike aught known before. Then will the will-to-good flower forth as understanding and understanding blossom as goodwill in men."

Training for new age
discipleship is provided
by the *Arcane School.*
The principles of the
Ageless Wisdom are
presented through esoteric
meditation, study and
service as a *way of life.*

Write to the publishers
for information.

INDEX

A

A.A.B. *See* Bailey, Alice A.
Action, 29, 31, 40, 101, 131
Activity —
 aspect, 62
 system, 66
Adams, Ansel, 93
Ageless Wisdom, 2, 89, 121, 122, 124, 201
Agni, Lord, 51, 95
 and kundalini, 53
 Lord of Fire, 54
 rules mental plane, 52
 transition into New Age, 53
Agni Yoga, 95, 123
Alchemy, 37
Alignment, 155, 229
Allied Forces, 187
Altruism, 34
Altruistic, 19
America, 47
Angel, 16, 43, 48-9
Angelic, 42
Anger, 29
Animals, 44
Antahkarana, 126, 179
Aquarian Age, 3, 10, 92, 102, 113, 127, 194
 and Christ, 114, 150, 152-3
 and Great Invocation, 115
 cycle of, 109-110, 147
 experience, 111
 group disciple, 214
 group pattern, 213
 groups, 100
 leadership, 212
 rays of, 198-9

training, 96
 yoga, 218
Arab, 161
Arcane School, 104
 and A.A.B., 10, 11
 building of, 14
 changes, 100
 experiment, 96
 financing of, 77-8
 group life-line, 2
 Mary Bailey's beginning with, 74
 objective, 126
 principles, 103
 requirements, 124-5
 students of, 12
 successor to head, 15
 useful, 124
Ashram, 23, 84, 92, 151, 211
 of K.H., 9
 of Sanat Kumara, 2
 second ray, 11
Ashramic
 need, 99
 pattern, 213-214, 220
 purpose, 99
Aspirant(s), 10, 89
Aspiration, 33, 61
Assagioli, Roberto, 196
Astral
 body, 15, 18, 29, 30-1, 33-4, 38-9, 40, 42, 44, 55
 clear, 42
 development, 26
 levels, 46, 65
 matter, 37
 plane, 21, 23, 37, 38, 44
 poise, 41
 psychism, 19

of energies behind
  Christ, 236
True, 35
Truth, 37, 56, 106
Tunbridge Wells, 74, 75, 82,
  85

U

Understanding, 236
United Nations, 134, 143,
  172, 187, 188
Unity, 34, 45, 67, 110, 112,
  132, 143-4, 172
    buddhic plane, 61
    create, 100
    internal, 25
    next manvantara, 65
Universality, 131-3
Universe, 45
Upanishads, 13
Usefulness, 120

V

Value(s), 43, 134, 227
    fate determined by, 135
    new, better, 145
    real, 187
    spiritual, 12, 132, 142
    undermined, 136
Varuna, 53
Vehicle(s), 21, 26-7, 29, 31-2,
  38, 39, 40, 48, 133
Vienna, 191
Vibration, 40, 41, 43, 44, 45,
  173
    at third initiation, 26
    high, 35, 36, 47
    light, 22
    lower, 42
    of astral, 29
    of ego, 28
    of Master, 24, 41
    of Presence, 34
    violent, 39, 42, 45
Violet, 32, 54

Virgo, 179
Vision
    circumscribed, 62
    devas, 51
    inner, 69
    sensed, 19
    wider, 42
Visualisation, 167
Visualise, 31, 32
Vitality, 38

W

War, 134-6
Wesak, 117, 222, 236
White Lodge, 181, 184
Whole, 28, 33, 121, 150, 193,
  218
Will, 33, 51, 155, 164, 167,
  233
    imposing, 216
    of God, 155, 172, 179,
      222, 225
    peaceful, silent, 201, 222,
      236
    sacrificial, 91
    to be, 225
    to good, 114, 116, 156,
      236
    to live, 225
    to love, 164
    to serve, 164
    synonyms, 225

X

Xhosa, 115

Y

Yanks, 73
Yellow, 58
Yoga, of synthesis, 218
    See also Agni, Raja.
Yoga Sutras of Patanjali, 13

Z

Zodiac, 109-110, 169, 178